MITCHAM

A PICTORIAL HISTORY

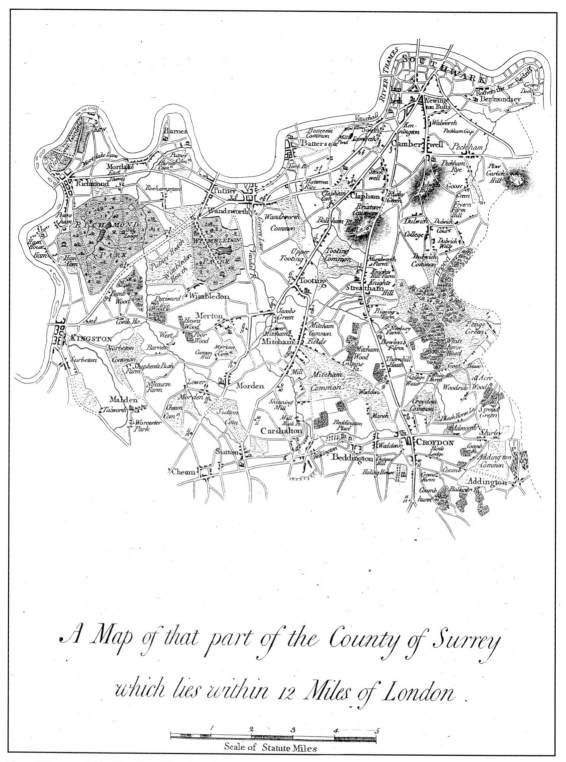

A Map of that part of the County of Surrey which lies within 12 Miles of London.

Scale of Statute Miles

Map of Surrey within 12 miles of London. (Engraving reproduced from Daniel Lysons' 'Environs of London', Volume I, published in 1792.) Mitcham can be seen as one of many villages scattered across the undeveloped countryside of north-east Surrey. Main routes out of London follow the line of old Roman roads, and place-names with Saxon origins show that the pattern of settlement pre-dated the Norman Conquest by at least three centuries. In the vicinity of Mitcham, open fields and common land are still dominant features of the landscape.

MITCHAM
A Pictorial History

Eric Montague

Phillimore

1991

Published by
PHILLIMORE & CO. LTD.
Shopwyke Hall, Chichester, Sussex

ISBN 0 85033 801 8

Printed and bound in Great Britain by
BIDDLES LTD.,
Guildford, Surrey

List of Illustrations

Frontispiece: N.E. Surrey in 1792

Acknowledgements

Whereas inevitably, in a work of this brevity, the omissions are many, I hope the factual errors are few. My greatest debt is to my wife, without whose meticulous checking and always helpful criticism the textual quality of this little offering would have been the poorer.

Retrospectively, gratitude must certainly be expressed to the committee of Merton Historical Society for their insistence that *Mitcham – A Brief History* should be written in the first place. I am also most grateful to Richard Milward and Clive Orton for their encouraging remarks on reading the first edition, published in paperback by Merton Historical Society in 1987, and to the staff of the Surrey Record Office, the Surrey Archaeological Society, the Surrey Room of the Minet Library, and of the borough libraries of Merton, Croydon, Wandsworth and Sutton for their unfailing courtesy and tolerance, without which the compilation of this history would have been impossible.

Finally, I wish to acknowledge the sources of the following illustrations, and to thank those concerned for in some cases entrusting original prints to Messrs. Phillimore for reproduction: the London Borough of Merton, the frontispiece, and illustrations numbered 1, 13, 14, 20, 22, 23, 25, 26, 29, 32, 37, 39, 40, 43, 46-52, 54-6, 58, 63, 67, 68, 71, 73, 79, 88, 89, 107,118-21, 131, 133, 141, 146-8, 151-4, 156; the London Borough of Wandsworth libraries, 69, 73, 94, 105, 106, 110, 124, 128, 130; the British Museum, 3, 5 and 6; the London Museum, 7 and 8; the City of London Guildhall library, 33 and 92; the Surrey Record Office, 52 and 108; the G.L.C. Historic Buildings Division, 45 and 102; Surrey Archaeological Society, 97; the London Borough of Sutton central library, 44, John Gent; 35, 72, 74, 86, 91, 99, 100, 113, 116-17, 123, 125, 134 and 137; and finally Roy Brown for the loan of his print of Pains Firework factory for illustration 87.

Introduction

Geographical Background

The village of Mitcham developed at the centre of a tract of fertile dark loam in the valley of the river Wandle, which had probably attracted settlement long before the Roman occupation of Britain. The strata underlying much of what was to become the ecclesiastical parish and ultimately the Borough of Mitcham are the sands and gravels of the Taplow Beds, ensuring both good subsoil drainage and a readily accessible supply of water from shallow wells. Much of the area is flat, but the land rises gently to the north-east. Immediately beyond the old parish boundaries the outcropping London Clay forms further low hills to the east and south-west.

The parish was probably established in the late Saxon period, its limits being to a large extent determined by natural features: the Wandle separating Mitcham from Carshalton and Morden to the south-west, and Merton and Wimbledon to the north-west, whilst its tributary, the Graveney, formed much of the boundary with the parishes of Tooting and Streatham to the north.

In extent, the parish measured two miles from east to west and three miles from north to south, covering 2,916 acres. Although it was subdivided for ecclesiastical purposes during the late 19th and early 20th centuries, the ancient parochial boundaries endured to become those of the Urban District of Mitcham in 1915, and finally the Borough of Mitcham, created when the rapidly growing town received its Charter in 1934.

The Prehistoric Period

Widespread cultivation over the last millennium, followed by gravel extraction and extensive urbanisation, have obliterated virtually all visual evidence for occupation prior to the early Middle Ages. As a result, our knowledge of Mitcham in the prehistoric and early historic periods is restricted to what we can deduce from the handful of remains discovered during gravel digging in the 19th century, and limited archaeological excavation in the 20th.

The first indication of human presence comes from the rough stone implements found in gravel pits during the last century. These Palaeolithic tools, sometimes lying in the same deposit as the remains of mammoth and other animals of the Pleistocene period, possibly date to the Hoxnian interglacial stage of $c.200,000$ B.C. Often worn and abraded, they are most likely to have been derived from gravels outside Mitcham, redistributed by ancient river systems.

Mesolithic hunting groups of the early post-glacial period ($c.8,500$ B.C. onwards) would have followed game through the increasingly wooded terrain of the valley floor, and fished in the Wandle. Unlike Carshalton and Wimbledon, Mitcham has not so far produced any substantial evidence of their presence. Neolithic flint hand axes or hoes from Mitcham imply that by about 3,000 B.C., if not before, land clearance and cultivation was already taking place with, presumably, settlement. From the late Bronze

Age of the last millennium B.C., we have a group of bronze axes discovered as a small hoard near Mitcham Junction Station *c*.1890, and evidence of a ditched enclosure off Western Road. Old maps of the Common mark a 'Maiden Hill' by Beddington Lane looking suspiciously like a Bronze Age tumulus, but this was levelled, probably during the construction of the golf-course.

It is likely that occupation of this part of the Wandle valley by farming communities continued into the pre-Roman Iron Age, but although again there is evidence from Wimbledon, Beddington and Wallington, virtually nothing has been reported from Mitcham. The only exception is a gold coin of Gallo-Belgic origin, dating to the period immediately prior to Caesar's expeditions of 55 and 54 B.C., found on an allotment on Mitcham Common in 1917.

The Roman and Early Saxon Periods

Settlement during the Roman period was evidently widespread in Mitcham, and whereas no actual buildings have been identified, occupational debris and burials have been found at various sites. Stane Street, an important element in the imperial road system, was probably constructed soon after the Conquest as part of the consolidation of Roman rule in the south-east, and linked the provincial capital of Londinium with Noviomagus Regnensium (Chichester), the newly-established tribal capital of the Atrebates under their king Cogidubnus. The road survives through Mitcham in the guise of Colliers Wood High Street. The actual point at which the Wandle was crossed has been lost, but on the western bank of the river, in the vicinity of Phipps Bridge, a small roadside settlement flourished throughout the Roman period.

To the south-east of this site, on what is now the playing field of Haslemere Primary School, ditches containing pottery dating to the first and second centuries were excavated in 1966 close to three undated burials. Still further to the south-east, when a gas holder was being constructed in 1882, a Roman well was discovered, containing at its bottom an intact jar of second-century date. Nearby there must have been another small settlement or farmstead but this has yet to be identified. Two inhumations, accompanied by a fine group of third/fourth-century pottery, were found in Willow Lane during gravel extraction in 1928, and further fragments of Romano-British pottery have come from archaeological excavations in the vicinity of the Upper Green, to the south of the parish church, and on the Watermeads housing estate.

Archaeology so far has nothing to tell us of the later Roman period in Mitcham, and we are left to assume continuity of small Romanised Celtic farmsteads into the late fourth and early fifth centuries. The relationship between these Romano-British people and the first Saxon migrants is unknown, but it is now believed that a substantial and distinct 'British' element could have survived in the locality until well into the seventh century or later.

The first evidence for Saxons in Mitcham comes from the famous cemetery which lay either side of the Morden Road, to the west of Mitcham Station. Some 230 burials were excavated between 1888 and the early 1920s, and probably as many again have been destroyed without record, or still remain undisturbed. A substantial number of the interments were of heavily-armed men and their womenfolk, the weapons, jewellery and pottery indicating dates from perhaps as early as 450, to about 600. The Mitcham cemetery is the largest of several known from around the eastern and southern outskirts of London, and it has been suggested that some of the earliest burials may have been of Anglo-Saxons encouraged to settle on the approaches to Londinium in the fifth century to protect the city, surrounding villages and farmsteads from surprise attack by seaborne raiders. A number of the pots and glass vessels from the Mitcham graves are in the late Romano-British tradition, whereas other grave goods, including pottery and personal jewellery, point to a north German ancestry of their owners. The evidence here, as elsewhere, certainly indicates a degree of cultural contact, if not actual ethnic fusion, between the native British and the newcomers.

The site of the early Saxon settlement at Mitcham is unknown and no evidence for the timber buildings which typify this period has been reported. The actual location of the main area of habitation of 'Micham' – as it was known by the seventh century – must therefore remain conjectural. It would have stood apart from the cemetery, but given normal settlement drift over the intervening centuries any one of several sites is a possibility. In some excavated examples Saxon houses and their outbuildings have been found grouped irregularly around a central open area. Such an arrangement could have existed at Mitcham in the vicinity of either of the two Greens. The fact that both are foci of road networks leading to other villages with names extant in the seventh or eighth centuries must be of significance. Unfortunately so far corroborative archaeological evidence is absent.

What may be the earliest documentary reference to Mitcham appears in a 13th-century transcript of a charter of the Benedictine abbey of St Peter at Chertsey, claimed to date from the early eighth century, confirming the royal grant of lands in north-east Surrey to the abbey soon after its foundation in 666. The siting of the parish church of Mitcham, close to the most northerly of the pagan Saxon graves to have been reported, suggests that after the final conversion of the community to Christianity a small chapel or preaching cross may have been set up, near land already hallowed by the burial of ancestors. Once again, the archaeological record is unhelpful, and even had an early church existed, it is unlikely to have survived the Danish raids of the ninth century. There is, moreover, no mention of a church at Mitcham in the Domesday Survey of 1086, but it must be said that such omissions are not uncommon, particularly when a church was small, or not well endowed.

The Late Saxon and Norman Periods
The impact upon Mitcham of the Norse invasions of the ninth and tenth centuries is difficult to assess, but Stane Street afforded easy access to the interior of Surrey and encouraged incursions into the surrounding countryside. Guthram's 'Great Army' invaded Wessex in 871, and was met by a force of Saxons under Alfred and his brother Ethelred at Meretune, which some authorities have identified as Merton. The Danes could not be held, and we can be sure the people of Mitcham, as well as the surrounding villages, would not have escaped unscathed. For seven years Surrey was under Danish rule, and peace did not return until the boundaries of Wessex and Danelaw were established in 879.

We know that by 967 what, a thousand years later, was still the boundary between the Borough of Mitcham and the Urban District of Merton and Morden was well established, for in that year a royal charter referred to it as 'Michamingemerke' – the boundary of the people of Mitcham. A century later there were six main estates in Mitcham, held by tenants of King Edward the Confessor. From a knowledge of the subsequent history of these holdings, we can say approximately where they were located. Britric, the major landholder, had some eight or nine hundred acres, probably in north and central Mitcham. Ledmer held a little over two hundred acres, and two further tenants, Edmer and Lank, had between them a total of about six hundred acres in Lower Mitcham. Two additional unnamed holdings held by tenants of Chertsey Abbey seem to have been located in north Mitcham and Colliers Wood. The use of the Wandle as a source of power can be traced to the late Saxon period, and two mills were operating at the time of King Edward. One may have been a little upstream from Mitcham Bridge, and the other in the vicinity of Phipps Bridge.

Major Saxon landholders had to serve their monarch in time of war, taking such men as could be spared from their labours to swell the fyrd or militia. We have no idea of the number of men raised in Mitcham, or how the little contingent fared in the battles at Stamford Bridge and Battle in 1066, but it is clear that the defeated Saxon landholders were dispossessed, for they had disappeared from the scene by the time of Domesday to be replaced by Norman nobles. Rewarded with English estates for their part in the Conquest, Bishop Odo of Bayeux, King William's half-brother, and William Fitz Ansculf, Sheriff of Surrey, controlled a substantial part of Mitcham by 1086, leasing holdings to various subtenants. In the case of Odo's property, the major portion was held by the canons of Bayeux.

The Domesday Survey found a community of some 250 people living in two separately identified 'vills' or hamlets, Mitcham and Whitford. No woodland is recorded, and we can assume the old wildwood or primeval forest had long been cleared. Some land was already held 'in demesne', that is, enclosed to form home farms, and there must also have been numerous scattered crofts or smallholdings, cultivated by individual villagers. By far the major part of the arable land would have been in the large open fields. Their precise extent is not known, but three, the West Field or 'Blacklands', the East Field and the South Field, are known from later records. The common pasture and wasteland of the parish, much of which still survives as public open space, comprised unenclosed tracts of open heath and scrub over which the villagers exercised various rights, including that of 'turning out' their livestock, and gathering fuel. It was in defence of this valuable resource that the villagers of Mitcham successfully joined forces with the prior of Merton in an action for trespass against the Huscarls, lords of the manor of Beddington, before the king's assize court in 1240.

The tenure of the canons of Bayeux did not long outlast the disgrace of Bishop Odo in 1088, and over the next two centuries the records show numerous changes in the possession of the Mitcham estates. There is evidence of some restitution of lands to their former owners after the accession of Henry I, notably to Robert, son of Wolfward, and Robert le Poure. Holding land by serjeanty, that is the performance of a duty to the Crown, they were responsible for providing a pound in which to hold goods and chattels seized by the king's officers as 'distresses', were charged with the duty of attendance at the king's court at Wallington, and of ensuring the transfer of prisoners to Guildford castle. There are also several instances in the 12th and 13th centuries of the granting of lands in Mitcham to the great priories of St Mary Overy at Southwark and Merton.

The Middle Ages
By the 13th century a considerable part of central Mitcham lay within the estate of Baldwin de Redvers (or 'de L'Isle'), Earl of Devon and Wight, as part of his manor of Vauxhall. Following a family tradition of ecclesiastical endowment, the advowson of Mitcham was granted to the priory of St Mary Overy in 1259, and it is most probably to the munificence of this family that we can attribute much of the fine Early English church which survived on the site of the present church until it was demolished in 1819.

From the late 13th century until the Dissolution in 1538, patronage of the church, and a considerable part of the parish – held as the manor of Mitcham Canons – was in the hands of the priory. With the tithes, it then passed into lay hands.

Towards the close of the Middle Ages the manorial system had become well established in Mitcham, and much of the parish fell within the jurisdiction of one or other of four manors, Biggin and Tamworth (substantially in north Mitcham), Vauxhall (extending from Phipps Bridge to Commonside West), Mitcham Canons and, mainly to the south and west of the parish, the manor of Ravensbury. The boundaries are now difficult to identify, and the lands held by the manors tended to be fragmented rather than grouped together in one part of the parish. The manors appear in the main to have had their origins in the separate estates identifiable at the time of the Conquest, but become more clearly discernible in records of the late 13th and early 14th centuries. Biggin and Tamworth was the latest to emerge by name, initially as an estate held by the prior of Merton. From the beginning of the 14th century the descent of the manors through various owners can be traced until the final extinction of manorial rights in the early years of this century. With the exception of Mitcham Canons, the court rolls of the manors survive almost intact from the later Middle Ages onwards, and are a valuable source of information. Mitcham Common fell within the claimed jurisdiction of all four Mitcham manors, and also of the manor of Beddington. Inability of the lords of these manors to agree on the precise extent of their interests fortunately resulted in Mitcham Common surviving the enclosure movement of the late 18th and early 19th centuries largely intact.

Although of course we cannot be certain, it would appear likely from study of the earliest maps that Mitcham had evolved as a 'polynucleated village', with various foci of settlement distributed around the Greens and elsewhere. Indeed, the first antiquarians and topographers customarily referred to it as a large and scattered village. In the vicinity of the parish church, perhaps due to the influence of the de Redvers, we can discern some evidence of planned development in the Middle Ages, typified by a row of long, narrow tenements extending from the street frontage to a back lane, beyond which lay the open West Field. Elsewhere the settlement pattern has the appearance of unplanned and haphazard growth, and includes the usual evidence of squatters' enclosures on the margins of the Common and various smaller parcels of parish wasteland.

Hardly any buildings survive from the medieval village; the dovecote in the Canons grounds bears the date 1511, and has the distinction of being the oldest complete structure still standing. Of the 13th-century parish church only the lower part of the tower was retained during reconstruction shortly after the end of the Napoleonic Wars. Old foundations, usually of flint and chalk, are uncovered from time to time during building works, as at Hall Place and on the site of Mitcham Grove. From watercolours and sketches we can gain some impression of what has been lost – notably Old Bedlam overlooking the Upper Green, with a first-floor hall and an undercroft, oriel windows, a wealth of chimneys, half-timbering and jettied upper floors, and Hall Place, which had a ground-floor hall open to the carved timbers of the roof, a private chapel dating to 1349, and jettied cross-wings added in the early Tudor period. Nothing remains above ground of the more humble cottages occupied by the great majority of the village people.

Fortunately we have information which enables us to form a picture of the lives of some of the more important people who lived in Mitcham during the Middle Ages. As early as the mid-14th century we can see evidence of Mitcham attracting merchants of the City of London, seeking country estates as an investment for their profits and as a means of attaining the higher social status that attached to the ownership of land. One of the first is Henry de Strete, a vintner, who acquired a substantial house and the lordship of the manor of Ravensbury shortly before the outbreak of the Black Death in 1348. Unfortunately for de Strete, the Black Prince's campaigns in northern France brought havoc to the vine-growing areas and disrupted the wine trade, and within 20 years we find him obliged firstly to mortgage his Mitcham estate, and then, in 1373, selling to the prior of Merton.

A contemporary of de Strete, and a first signatory of his mortgage in 1357, was William Mareys, a member of the influential de la Mere family who had held land in the parish, including a farm at Ravensbury, since the middle of the previous century. Another signatory was William Figge, holding land in sergeanty as Robert son of Wolfward had two hundred years before. Figge's lands and responsibilities descended to his son, another William, before passing out of the family. Their connection with Mitcham is perpetuated in Figge's Marsh, a tract of former common grazing land in north Mitcham, now preserved as public open space.

Tudors and Stuarts

The dissolution of the monasteries in 1538 and the disposal of the Mitcham estates held by the priories of Southwark and Merton was followed by the emergence of new landowners, and the transfer of the lordships of the manors of Mitcham Canons and Biggin and Tamworth. Ravensbury was already in secular hands, but Vauxhall remained in the possession of the Church, the dean and chapter of Canterbury continuing as lords of the manor over a considerable part of central Mitcham, including the Lower and Cricket Greens, for another four centuries.

The parish registers of Mitcham, recording the baptisms, marriages and burials of the villagers, start from the mid-16th century, providing an extremely valuable and reliable source of information about Mitcham people. In part they were published with biographical notes by Robert Garroway Rice, a barrister and local antiquary, whose researches in the 19th century greatly increased our knowledge of the history of Mitcham. The vestry minutes and other local government records, further important sources of local history material, do not survive from before the mid-17th century, the earliest being the churchwardens' accounts for part of the Commonwealth period.

Thus from the latter part of the 16th century we not only have personal data for the first time relating to the ordinary people of Mitcham, but also increasing information about the more important residents. We can, furthermore, begin to understand how the village came to be renowned for its good company. It was situated a little over an hour's drive from the capital and, most importantly for those seeking royal preferment, within a short distance of the royal palaces at Richmond, Nonsuch and Greenwich. Moreover, it acquired a reputation for its fresh air and pure water – both scarce in Tudor London. As a result the village attracted many connected with the court and government, as well as those with legal practices or commercial interests in the City of London.

The first of many such families one could mention were the Illingworths. Sir Richard Illingworth, Chief Baron of the Exchequer under Edward IV, and member of parliament for Nottingham in 1457 and 1476, owned a house in Mitcham which can be identified with Hall Place. Three generations of Illingworths lived in the village and, with responsibility for the upkeep of the north chancel of the parish church, they were interred in the lady chapel there. Their fine monuments, mutilated probably during the Commonwealth, have now disappeared after removal during the rebuilding of the church in 1819-21.

By the second half of the 16th century Mitcham's more notable residents included Nicholas Rutland, Clerk to the Catery (a department of the royal household), Thomas Smythe, Clerk of the Greencloth (another department of the Crown), Sir Thomas Blanke, Lord Mayor of London in 1582, and Sir Nicholas Throgmorton. The Carews of Beddington held the manor of Ravensbury, and in 1544 lordship of Biggin and Tamworth was granted to Robert Wilford, citizen and merchant taylor of London, whose widow became Lady Mordaunt of Drayton. Mitcham Canons passed into the possession of Nicholas Spakman and Christopher Harebottel, haberdashers of London, in 1545 and to Richard Burton of Beddington in 1589.

Elizabeth Throgmorton, maid of honour to Queen Elizabeth I, who married Sir Walter Raleigh, owned property in Mitcham which was sold when funds were raised to finance Sir Walter's disastrous expedition to the Orinoco river in 1616. The courtier and poet John Donne, who became dean of St Paul's in 1621, lived from 1605 to 1611 in a little house in Mitcham. His remorseful letters survive, complaining of the damp and cold to which his children and ailing wife, a daughter of Sir George More of Losely, were subjected whilst he sought a patron. A far wealthier man, Julius Caesar Adelmare, judge in the Court of Admiralty, acquired a large mansion in Lower Mitcham on marrying Alice, the widow of John Dent, a wealthy London merchant, and had the honour of playing host to the Queen in 1598. Queen Elizabeth in fact visited Mitcham on no fewer than five separate occasions, staying twice with Alice Dent before her remarriage, and twice with Margaret Lady Blanke. Julius Caesar Adelmare was knighted by James I in 1603, became Chancellor of the Exchequer in 1606 and Master of the Rolls in 1614.

Towards the end of the 16th century Mitcham had become the home of several refugee families seeking freedom from religious persecution in the Spanish Netherlands. To them can be attributed the introduction of the trade of whitstering, or the bleaching of linens, which became an important local industry, dependent on the pure waters of the Wandle and on its watermeadows, where the washed fabrics were spread to bleach and dry in the sun. One of these families, the Collandes, had bleaching grounds off the Carshalton Road, near *The Goat*, beginning a long tradition of industry in this part of Mitcham. Attempts to enclose the South Field – probably to increase the extent of the bleaching grounds – met with strong opposition, and a group of 27 Mitcham people successfully appealed to Charles I in privy council in 1637 for their common rights to be preserved. The king's father, James I, had been less sympathetic to local customs when it came to safeguarding sporting rights in the district, and appointed bailiffs on the Wandle to curb the poaching of trout for which the river was renowned.

The Civil War

The commencement of civil war in 1642 found Mitcham a prosperous agricultural village, still surrounded by its open fields in strip cultivation, its extensive commons and water meadows. Much land had long since been taken into private tenure, either as parkland, gardens or small farms. Most of the oak woodland which once covered the heavier clay in the extreme east and south-east of the parish had been felled, and the hedged fields of farms like New Barns were extending from the Common north-eastwards towards the Streatham boundary. Only Mitcham Great Wood, on the slopes of Pollards Hill, remained, and charcoal burners had disappeared in all but name from Colliers Wood.

The nearest outbreak of fighting to Mitcham appears to have been a skirmish at Ewell in 1648, but the village was affected indirectly by the war in various ways. Some of the local gentry rallied to the Royalist cause, like young Robert Howard, knighted at the age of 18 for bravery on the field at Newbury, and afterwards imprisoned in Windsor Castle by the Parliamentary forces. Others endeavoured to avoid the conflict and to survive. The lawyer Richard Farrand moved with his family to Oxford to escape continual harassment at the hands of Cromwell's troops quartered in the district, only to find himself facing excessive demands for money from the Royalists. Merton Priory was garrisoned by Parliament, and many villagers must have suffered enforced billeting of troops and the seizure of produce and livestock. Years later the body of a 'colonel in Cromwell's army' is said to have been found buried in the garden of a 17th-century house off Lower Green West, and one wonders at the circumstances leading to his death. Sir Robert Tichborne, a signatory of Charles I's death warrant in 1649, was resident in Mitcham for several years, living in the house formerly owned by Sir Julius Caesar. He left the village shortly before the Restoration, and was soon to be tried and imprisoned for life in the Tower, where he died in 1682.

Changes in land ownership during the Civil War and the Commonwealth were to be expected – financial ruin, for instance, enforced the sale of the Mitcham estate of Sir Henry Burton of Carshalton – and we find new people coming to the village. Typical was Robert Cranmer, a London merchant whose family claimed descent from Archbishop Cranmer, martyred at the stake in 1556. Robert Cranmer was in the East Indies for much of the earlier part of the war, and had returned to England in 1647 a wealthy man. Within six years he purchased the manor of Mitcham Canons, Sir Robert Howard's former house, and much of the old Burton estate, and settled in Mitcham with his young wife.

Tragically, in 1665, the year of the great plague, Robert and Mary Cranmer died, leaving the estate in trust for their seven young sons. Cranmer's death brought to an end an acrimonious dispute with the vicar, Anthony Sadler, a Royalist supporter whom he had appointed to the living at Mitcham in 1661. The dispute is well documented in contemporary pamphlets, and throws an interesting light on what must have been a very difficult period for the village.

Restoration and Early Georgian Mitcham

The Cranmer family and their descendants, the Simpsons, held the manor of Mitcham and an extensive estate in the parish for nearly three centuries, a period from which many of the family papers and records survive. From them, for instance, we learn of the building lease granted by John Cranmer in 1680 for the Canons house, which survives today.

With the Restoration a new era began in Mitcham, dubbed 'The Montpelier of England' by an eminent physician of the day on account of its fine air. The village continued to attract the wealthy, notably London merchants and lawyers seeking a healthy residence away from the perpetual threat of plague in London. Eagle House, one of Mitcham's finest houses, dates from this period, being built, it is believed, in 1705 for Fernando Mendez, physician to Queen Catherine, wife of Charles II, and later occupied by Sir James Dolliffe, a director of the ill-fated South Sea Company.

By the 1660s Epsom had already become a spa much favoured by Londoners, and the improvement in the roads, which was to reach a peak under the turnpike trusts a century later, meant that coach travel became easier and faster. The growth of wayside inns reflects this greater mobility, and several Mitcham hostelries can be either dated to the middle of the 18th century, or were refurbished at this time. The earliest surviving inn, the former *King's Head* (recently renamed the *Burn Bullock* in memory of a popular cricketing licencee) dates in part to the late 16th or early 17th century, as its timbered rear part indicates. The front, however, is Georgian, improved or 'modernised' in about

1760 to compete with the *White Hart* opposite, which had been substantially rebuilt in 1750. Old records and prints show the former *Buck's Head* and the old *Five Bells* at Colliers Wood also to have been buildings typical of the mid-18th century. The latter was named after the ring of bells carried by the leading horses of the wagoners, who used the forecourt of the inn as a regular stopping place to offload and pick up goods. In addition to providing refreshment and lodgings for travellers, the inns also catered for the horses.

The *White Hart* was a posting house, from which post chaises and mounts could be hired, and from the stables at the rear Mitcham's first horse bus service was run by the Holden family. Even before the Napoleonic Wars, stage coaches were leaving for London at half-hourly intervals during the morning and evening 'rush hours', reaching Gracechurch Street within the hour.

The high roads from London to Brighton, via Tooting and Sutton, and another through Colliers Wood to Epsom, were turnpiked in about 1747, under an act of 1734/5. The trusts operated a tollgate at Figges Marsh and another at Colliers Wood (the 'Single Gate') raising money for road maintenance. They were abolished in 1865, when the condition of the main roads became the responsibility of elected local boards, and all that remains to recall the trusts are the milestones they erected in about 1755 – one surviving at Figges Marsh, near the site of the old gate, and another, inscribed 'Whitehall 8½ mls Royal Exchange 9 mls' at Lower Green West.

The Changing Economy

The activity for which Mitcham was best known in the 18th and 19th centuries was the cultivation of medicinal and aromatic herbs and the distillation of essences and perfumes. The industry had its origins in the 14th century, when Merton priory's Biggin estate grew 'spikings' or lavender, and 'physic gardeners' are known in Mitcham from the early 18th century. It was not, however, until 1749 that distillation of lavender water commenced on an industrial scale, the innovators being Ephraim Potter and William Moore. Although lavender was to become synonymous with Mitcham, it was actually exceeded in commercial importance by peppermint, the oil of which was much in demand from the makers of cordial waters as well as apothecaries in the 18th and 19th centuries. The rich dark loam, particularly in the western part of Mitcham, and the dry gravelly soils to be found elsewhere in the parish, favoured the growth of a variety of other herbs, including camomile, wormwood, aniseed, damask roses and liquorice. Expansion of the industry was rapid, and whereas in the 1750s only a small acreage was used for herb growing, 250 acres of physic grounds existed in 1796. By 1802 a further 240 acres of meadow, pasture and arable land had been taken over, including much of the open common fields. Topographical writers at the turn of the century invariably commented on the extent and beauty of the herb gardens where, it was said, the art of cultivation had been brought to a state of perfection unrivalled in the kingdom. Hassell, the watercolour artist, described the colours in late summer as 'particularly diversified', the blue from the ripe lavender, and the red and brown from the ripe herbs contrasting with the golden yellows of the cereals and the purple of the seed clovers.

Potter and Moore's distillery, in its time a show-place of Mitcham, stood to the north of the present *Swan* Inn, overlooking Figges Marsh. Here could be seen the great copper stills used in the process of extracting essential oils from a host of different plants, fed by one of the district's first recorded artesian wells, tapping water in the chalk over 200 ft. below ground level. Many such wells came to be sunk in the next century-and-a-half, supplying some of the larger houses, and industries as diverse as brewing and soft drink manufacture, milk bottling, butter and margarine processing, and the production of sugar confectionery and paints. As the extraction rate increased, so the water level dropped, and pumps had to be installed eventually to raise the water to the surface.

It was during the 18th century that the textile processing industries in the Wandle valley reached new heights of prosperity, and from Carshalton to Wandsworth the 'whitsters', or bleachers, colour mills, and printing and dye works along the river banks flourished in response to the demands of fashion for coloured and printed chintzes and calicos. To a great extent production in the early years was in the hands of Huguenot families like the Mauvillains and Haultains, but as the century progressed the industry expanded, and men like Selby, Foster Reynolds, Rucker and Arbuthnot rose to prominence in the Mitcham area. Large bleaching and printing works came to be established at Willow Lane, Ravensbury and Phipps Bridge, employing a considerable number of hands. The peak of production was reached around the turn of the century, and thereafter changes in fashion, and above all growing competition from the industrial north of England, brought several of the Mitcham manufacturers to bankruptcy. A few survived into the mid-19th century, relying mainly on serving the luxury market in London for printed silks and other fine fabrics, but all the Mitcham mills had ceased production by the 1870s.

Snuff milling was another local industry dependent on the power of the Wandle and vulnerable to changes in social customs. One of the first to venture into this field in Mitcham seems to have been a member of the Arnold family, who was operating a snuff mill at Ravensbury in the 1750s. The mill passed through various hands until 1805, when it was taken over by John Rutter, a London tobacco and snuff manufacturer. The firm continued in Mitcham until about 1925. Another Mitcham snuff miller, Richard Glover, had been in the flour milling business since about 1774, taking over mills with a very long history. By 1795 one of his three mills by Mitcham Bridge was grinding snuff, and another was converted by 1805. Under his son the business failed in 1835.

Mitcham, always a populous parish, was fortunate at this time of expansion and change to have as residents men like James Cranmer and William Tate, both of whom were London attorneys, and later James Moore, a major farmer and grower of medicinal herbs, willing to devote themselves to supervising the conduct of local affairs. As a result the Webbs, the historians of English local government, instanced Mitcham Vestry as a model of conscientious parish administration. When the need arose for expert advice the Vestry, an elected and largely amateur body, with only its clerk and the parish beadle as paid officers, could call on several distinguished parishioners, who readily gave their services. Thus no less a person than the Chief Justice of Common Pleas, Lord Loughborough, could be consulted in 1782 and again the following year when a legal view was required. A few years later Henry Hoare, senior partner of Hoares Bank, was ready to guide the Vestry on financial matters, and often served on special committees.

The Vestry minutes show how the parish struggled through the latter half of the 18th and early 19th centuries to provide for the poor, educating orphaned children in its care and placing them with employers, and generally endeavouring to alleviate hardship with what seems to have been true compassion. A large workhouse for the destitute and homeless was built on the Common in 1782, surrounded by vegetable and flower gardens, and an infirmary for the sick and elderly was added in 1793, furnished by Henry Hoare at his own expense. The Vestry was in the forefront of the successful resistance to enclosure of the Common, proposed by local lords of the manors during the Napoleonic Wars, arguing that the preservation of rough grazing and the right to gather furze and turves, on which many of the poor depended for fuel, was essential for the economic well-being of the parish.

Henry Hoare is particularly worthy of a place in the history of Mitcham. Born in 1750, he became senior partner of the family bank in 1787, a position he was to hold until his death in 1828. He moved to Mitcham with his wife in 1786, purchasing the Mitcham Grove estate from Lord Loughborough who, as Alexander Wedderburn K.C., had been rewarded with the property following his brilliant defence of Clive of India at his impeachment in 1773. The estate included a beautiful house on the banks of the Wandle, surrounded by lawns and shrubberies, dating substantially from the mid-18th century, although it was on the foundations of the Elizabethan house once owned by the Smythe family.

Henry Hoare, a prominent member of the evangelical Clapham sect, numbered amongst his friends social reformers like Hannah More and William Wilberforce. He took a great interest in the affairs of Mitcham parish church, and was a trustee of the Sunday school, opened in 1788. When in 1811 it was proposed that a day school should be established under the auspices of the National Schools Society of the Church of England, it was only to be expected that Henry Hoare should become the treasurer, and his name can still be seen on the commemorative tablet above the door of the old school building overlooking Lower Green West. The seriously dilapidated condition of the fabric of the parish church had been a source of debate in Vestry for forty years when, in 1819, a decision was finally reached to demolish the church and rebuild. Again, Henry Hoare's advice and guidance were invaluable in raising the necessary finance for what was the most expensive enterprise hitherto undertaken by the Vestry.

The Napoleonic Wars and Their Aftermath

The Napoleonic Wars affected Mitcham in various ways. Recruitment to the militia and the navy, or the finding of substitutes, were major and recurrent problems, and the Vestry was repeatedly in difficulty in providing men to fill the quotas, or in raising money to pay the fines for non-compliance. The financial burden on the ratepayers was increased further by the steadily rising poor rate, the Vestry being obliged not only to pay out-relief to the aged and infirm, and the families of men serving in the forces, but also to augment the wages of the lower-paid village labourers, hard pressed by rising prices. Resourceful as ever, the Vestry started an experimental day school of industry in 1801, taking selected children from the Sunday schools. Wholesome meals were provided, and practical skills taught. It was hoped that sales of work would defray the running costs, but the school had to be subsidised, and the experiment seems to have been abandoned after five years or so. When in 1806 consideration was given to an application made to the manor of Biggin and Tamworth for licence to enclose part of the Common for the erection of a windmill, the Vestry saw another opportunity for helping the poor, and stipulated as a condition of their assent that the miller should on one day a week in perpetuity grind the villagers' corn at a fair price.

The records of the Loyal Mitcham Volunteer Infantry Corps make fascinating reading, and one can sense some of the patriotic fervour with which the villagers armed themselves to defend hearth and home against the expected invasion by 'Old Boney'. The Corps was formed in 1803, and raised three companies of 60 men each under the command of James Moore. Although formally enrolled under the Defence Acts, and liable to serve anywhere in the kingdom in the event of an emergency, the Corps retained a measure of independence, resolving not to accept pay and allowances from the Government for uniforms or 'contingencies'. Like the Home Guard a century and a half later, the Corps drilled and manoeuvred with a pride and determination that boded ill for any invader. Happily its members were never put to the test, and the Corps was disbanded in 1813.

Elementary education for the village children took a great step forward with the foundation of the National Schools in 1812. The upper classes had long been accustomed to making private provision for the education of their children, and in the late 18th century several of the larger houses in Mitcham came to be used as boarding academies for the sons and daughters of the gentry. The boys at one of these establishments, the Baron House Academy in Lower Mitcham, had the thrill of performing before Admiral Lord Nelson and his house guests from Merton Place shortly before Christmas 1801. Their master, James Dempster, specialised in training young men for careers in the armed forces or commerce, whilst at the Revd. Richard Roberts' academy at Glebelands many of the pupils progressed to Eton and the universities, ultimately following careers of distinction in government, the diplomatic corps, or the Church. Typical of those attending the school during the wartime years were Edward Stanley, later the 14th Earl of Derby, Prime Minister in 1851 and 1858, and Robert Eden, who became the Bishop of Bath and Wells and third Baron Auckland.

As we have seen, for centuries the Wandle had been used as a source of power, and alongside the textile processing works in the latter part of the 18th century there were flour, paper and snuff mills. The industries were thriving, but inevitably their expansion was restricted by the limited amount of water in the river. Steam power was becoming available, but needed coal, the transport of which overland was prohibitively expensive. The prospect of profit from serving the numerous factories, coupled with the need to establish safe overland transport between London and Portsmouth after the outbreak of war with France in 1793, prompted investigation by William Jessop, the civil engineer, into the possibility of constructing a canal from the Thames at Wandsworth along the Wandle valley and thence across Sussex. The canal project was abandoned in 1799 as impracticable, Jessop's report showing that the extraction of water needed for the canal would be opposed by the owners of the many mills who relied upon the river for power. As a result, in 1800 the idea of an iron rail road was adopted, to be operated on the toll principle already employed with success by the turnpike trusts.

The Surrey Iron Railway, the first public railway in the world, was authorised by Parliament in 1801, and the line from Wandsworth to Croydon was opened in 1803. The track through Mitcham ran along what is now Christchurch Road and Church Road, alongside Tramway Path, and across Mitcham Common. A toll gate was situated at Colliers Wood, and the Sutton to Mitcham road was crossed 'on the level'. A branch line ran to Hackbridge, and provision was made for another along Phipps Bridge Road. Traction was by horses or mules which, because of the very even gradient, were able to pull a considerable number of wagons. Passengers were never intended, and the main traffic was in the conveyance of coal from Wandsworth, and corn, chalk and lime from the Croydon and Merstham termini. The structure of the former Mitcham station (closed in 1989) is contemporary with the Surrey Iron Railway, but their often-claimed association is dubious. Nearby, however, at the corner of Tramway Path, is a one-time coal order office which was in existence before the railway was closed down in 1846. The Surrey Iron Railway, a unique experiment in transport and a pioneer of the modern railway system, was never a financial success. It failed to compete effectively with road transport and collapsed with the advent of the steam-powered railways, which began expanding rapidly in the 1830s and '40s.

In spite of war, inflation and rising taxation the period 1793-1815 was one of general prosperity. The farms and mills at Mitcham prospered, the population increased by 20 per cent between 1801 and 1811, and elegant villas in the new Regency style appeared in various parts of the village. In contrast, the aftermath of Waterloo found Mitcham, like the rest of Britain, in economic depression. Three of the larger estates, Colliers Wood, Biggin Grove and The Firs, were auctioned in 1822, and bankruptcies became common amongst the calico printers, many hands being laid off. Between 1821 and 1831 the population actually fell by 66 to 4,387.

A feature of the time, however, seems to have been the attitude of independence and self-help. Evening classes for adults were started in 1816; benefit societies flourished, providing elementary insurance against hard times; there were shoe, coal and clothing clubs encouraging thrift, and a local savings bank. The local gentry, employers of many villagers either directly in service, or indirectly as tradespeople, were also active in philanthropic activities to alleviate the lot of the poor. The Tate Almshouses overlooking the Cricket Green date from this period, the land being given and a charitable trust for their upkeep established by Miss Mary Tate in 1828.

The Victorian Period

The mid-Victorian period was recalled with obvious nostalgia by a number of old Mitcham residents who recorded their memories in the 1920s. Cricket was the great game, played on the Lower Green by all classes. Mitcham vied with Hambledon for the distinction of being the cradle of club cricket in the 18th century, and by the 1830s and '40s could field a team fit to take on all comers. The annual fair, held on 12, 13 and 14 August on the Upper Green, was regarded as an event of considerable antiquity and looked forward to by many. Attempts at suppression by the local justices in the 1770s had failed, and the fair remained the principal event in the Mitcham calendar throughout the 19th century, although increasingly it was seen as an intolerable nuisance by those in authority. Mitcham at this time seems never to have missed an opportunity to celebrate, be it a royal wedding or jubilee, or an apparently mundane occasion like the donation of a steam fire engine to the village brigade. Seasonal events like May Day or Guy Fawkes night were observed with enthusiasm, and Derby Day virtually brought normal life to a standstill with everyone turning out to watch the cavalcade of racegoers passing through on their way to and from the Epsom Downs.

Gipsies, attracted by the fair and the prospect of employment in the herb gardens, came to Mitcham in droves after the Epsom races. Dozens of their colourful caravans and tents could often be seen on the Common, where they made their own entertainment with impromptu horse racing and bare knuckle fights. Many were to settle in Mitcham, finding permanent sites for their vans in the yards off Western Road, and in the neighbourhood of Phipps Bridge, nicknamed 'Redskin Village'.

Until the mid-19th century Mitcham was skirted by the expanding railway network. The line from Wimbledon to Croydon was opened in 1855, to be joined by the line connecting Streatham and Sutton in 1868. Whereas Wimbledon and Croydon thus received a stimulus to suburban expansion in the early Victorian period, Mitcham did not, and what is more, failed to retain its popularity amongst the wealthier classes, attracting instead more than its fair share of somewhat offensive industries. Paint, varnish and linoleum manufactures, employing extremely noxious processes, came to be located to the west of the village centre, and a gas-works was established amongst the lavender fields off Western Road in 1849. Even the distillation of essential oils could be overpowering in the vicinity of the physic farms. Older Mitcham families like the Simpsons, and newer residents like the Boyd Millers at Colliers Wood, provided a stabilising element, but change was inevitable.

Although there were other 'physic' gardeners in Mitcham, like James Arthur of New Barns Farm, the great name in the herbal industry for much of the 19th century was undoubtedly that of James Moore. In 1805 the family firm of Potter and Moore had over 500 acres under cultivation, the major part as herb gardens. Moore was an outstanding figure in the village for over half a century. Major Commandant of the local defence forces, he acquired the lordship of the manor of Biggin and Tamworth in 1806, and played a prominent part in local government until his death at the age of 81 in 1851. Increasing competition from growers abroad, the rising demand for land brought about by improvements in public transport, and the relentless spread of London into the suburbs combined to bring about the eventual collapse of the Mitcham herbal industry, and the Potter and Moore estate was broken up and sold in 1886. A handful of minor growers survived into the 1900s, turning their land over more and more to horticulture, cultivating vegetables, cut flowers and plants for the London markets. Best known were the Mizen family, who until the 1950s worked the old east field from their farm in Grove Road, where they maintained extensive greenhouses. Supplying another need were the watercress farms along the banks of the Wandle. Names here included E. James and Sons, whose 'Vitacress' from the Brookfields Nurseries was well known and, of course, the Mizens who grew watercress in the Mitcham Junction area.

Despite the spread of new 'byelaw' housing, particularly in the neighbourhoods of Colliers Wood and Tooting Junction, and the undoubted existence of pockets of slums, Mitcham in the closing years of the 19th century was still an extremely pretty village, with a strong sense of community amongst its inhabitants. Quaint old weatherboarded and pantiled cottages abounded, and houses in mellow red brick and tile from the 18th century stood shoulder to shoulder with the later yellow stock brick and slate-roofed villas of the railway era. Here and there old mansions, set in cedar-shaded lawns, could be glimpsed through wrought-iron gates in long brick walls. The flower farms, the Wandle and the broad expanse of the Common – a typical Surrey heath extending to the Croydon boundary, with views to the hills of Norwood and, to the south, the Downs – were often described by the writers of guides and travel books.

The 19th century in Mitcham, as indeed elsewhere, was notable for the growth in the Free Church and Non-conformist movement. Another phenomenon, a consequence of the increase in population, was the division by the Church of England of the old ecclesiastical parish into new, smaller parishes, served by their own church buildings. Wesley had preached in Mitcham as early as 1764, and the first Wesleyan Methodist chapel had been opened on the Cricket Green in 1789. Zion Chapel, serving a congregation of 'Independent Calvinists', opened in 1819, and the first Baptist church in 1882. Roman Catholics, supported by the Simpson family who were actually patrons of the Anglican Church in Mitcham, had a chapel at the Cricket Green from 1861. Congregations in the latter half of the 19th century were large, reinforced by children from the Sunday schools and the private boarding academies. Church-going was, of course, fashionable at this time amongst the local gentry and prosperous tradespeople, and it was a common sight to see a line of carriages and horses waiting outside the parish church for the service to end. In the main the poor seem not to have been greatly motivated, and it was to bring the Gospel message to them and particularly to their children that both the Non-conformists and the established Church opened numerous mission halls, often in slum areas like Rock Terrace and Half Acre Row. These evangelising efforts were augmented by the Quaker community in Mitcham, the Band of Hope and the temperance societies, all of whom strove valiantly to bring godliness and sobriety to the 'working classes'. In 1875 a new Anglican parish of Christ Church, Colliers Wood, was created, followed by that of St Barnabas in North Mitcham in 1906 and St Mark in 1909. Parish reorganisation mirrored the continuing urbanisation of Mitcham, and the process was to be carried forward in the 1920s and '30s with the formation of the parishes of St Olave and the Church of the Ascension to serve the spiritual needs of the new estates then being developed towards Pollards Hill.

The growing importance of local government, still largely in the hands of the Vestry, was reflected in the erection of the red brick Vestry Hall on Lower Green West in the Jubilee year of 1887. The architect was Robert Masters Chart, great-grandson of William Chart, who had been appointed Vestry Clerk in 1761. His grandfather, John Chart, local builder and undertaker, had also been Vestry Clerk as had his father Edwin, by profession a surveyor. The Chart family's history of continuous service to the local community is quite extraordinary and probably unique, extending over 200 years. Robert Masters Chart was elected Mayor of Mitcham in 1934 at the age of 84, and his son, Colonel Stephen Chart, D.S.O., was Town Clerk until retirement in 1946.

The Vestry Hall, erected on the site of the village 'cage' or lock-up, the stocks and the pound, stood on common land within the manor of Vauxhall. Permission to enclose a plot 12 ft. by 20 ft. for the building of the lock-up had been granted in 1765 by the dean and chapter of Canterbury, lords of the manor, and further permission was duly obtained for an extension of the land taken in the interests of public service in 1887. The fire station of 1927 and the 'temporary' war-time council offices followed suit, also being justified by the common need, but the origins of the enclosure on which *The Cricketers* public house now stands are obscure.

The provision of public education was transformed by the Forster Act of 1870, and for the first time elementary day schooling became available to all. Schools established by the local school board opened at Singlegate, Colliers Wood in 1874, and at Mitcham in 1884 and 1897. The great workhouse complex established off Western Road by the Holborn Poor Law Union had its own schools – the Holborn Schools in London Road, famous for its excellent boys' band, much in demand at summer fêtes and village celebrations. In 1906 secondary education became the responsibility of Surrey County Council, and Mitcham County School for Boys (1922) and Mitcham County School for Girls (1929) were established.

Urban Mitcham

In the first decade of the 20th century the population of Mitcham doubled, reaching 29,606 in 1911. The growth of civic awareness, and the increasing complexity of local government, called for an advance in administrative status, and the area of the ancient medieval parish was created an Urban District in 1915. Surrey County Council retained responsibility for several major functions, including main roads and education, but Mitcham acquired considerable autonomy.

The Great War of 1914-18 took a heavy toll of its youth, and the names of many Mitcham men and boys are inscribed on the war memorial erected on the Lower Green. One of the first to fall had been Lt. William Mostyn Simpson of the East Surrey Regiment, eldest child of the lord of the manor of Mitcham, mortally wounded at Wolferghem in Belgium.

The war also brought about changes in social attitudes, which meant that the old Mitcham, dominated by the squire and a few long-established families, could never return. The new Urban District was enthusiastic in its support of the movement to provide 'homes for heroes' as soon as the Armistice was declared. Large estates of municipal cottage housing were built in the early '20s, notably on the Bordergate Estate to the west of Figges Marsh, with roads named after the aromatic herbs – lavender, camomile and roses – grown in the old physic gardens. Local benefactors contributed generously towards the developing townscape – Thomas Mason, the Tamworth Recreation Ground (1923), Sir Isaac Wilson, the Wilson Memorial Hospital (1928) and Mitcham Garden Village for the elderly (1929-32), and Joseph Owen, the Public Library (1933).

The building of council dwellings was matched by the appearance of huge estates of private housing, developed by firms like the Tamworth Park Construction Company, Wates of Norbury and New Ideal Homes of Epsom, and by the late 1930s much of Mitcham was covered by bricks and mortar. Open spaces were preserved, however, including Ravensbury Park, (managed jointly with the Urban District Council of Merton and Morden), disused gravel pits were reclaimed to became sports fields and numerous small recreation grounds were scattered amongst the new housing estates.

After a period of abuse and neglect, during which Mitcham Common suffered much at the hands of the railway companies, and was extensively dug for sand and gravel, its future had been safeguarded by the Metropolitan Commons (Mitcham) Supplemental Act of 1891 and management was placed in the hands of a Board of Conservators. In 1923 under a private Act the Urban District Council assumed control of Figges Marsh, the Upper (or Fair) Green, the Lower and Cricket Greens, Cranmers Piece and Three Kings Piece. At the same time the fair was moved from its traditional site to the Three Kings Piece, thus easing an annual traffic problem which had become intolerable.

The tramways had been extended from Tooting to Croydon via the Fair Green by 1906 and from Tooting to Wimbledon through Colliers Wood in 1907. The extension of the Northern line of London's Underground to Tooting and Morden in 1926 added greatly to the ease with which commuters could reach London and the City, and Mitcham steadily acquired the role of a dormitory suburb. The growing township was granted borough status in 1934 and by 1939 Mitcham was famous for its paint industry, and for a multitude of factories producing sugar confectionery, fireworks, bakery products, flavouring essences, milk and dairy products and tobacco, all with national brand names. Despite this rapid urbanisation, strong local traditions persisted, often fostered by pride in the new borough status. Many old residents still recall with nostalgia not only the fair, officially opened by the mayor in full regalia, holding aloft a large key, but also the annual carnival and fête held at Mitcham Stadium in aid of the Wilson Hospital, Gilbert and Sullivan operettas performed at the new Baths Hall by the boys of Mitcham County School, the Whitsun Walk around the Lower Green, and the crowning of the May Queen.

Within a year of the outbreak of World War Two in 1939 Mitcham, with other south London suburbs, found itself in the front line during the Battle of Britain. Heavily bombed during both day and night raids, the damage to houses and factories, and the loss of life, were severe. Casualties were not confined to the civilian population, and the auxiliary forces, notably the Civil Defence, the Home Guard and the Auxiliary Fire Service, suffered many killed or injured. In one tragic incident in April 1941, 15 members of 'B' Company 57th Surrey (Mitcham) Home Guard, on duty at the Tower Creameries, were killed by a parachute mine that fell on the factory. A large anti-aircraft battery was established in a hutted encampment near Mitcham Junction station, and public air raid shelters and emergency static water tanks were to be seen everywhere. Vacant housing was given 'first aid' repair and requisitioned for the homeless, whilst bombed sites sprouted Nissen huts for temporary accommodation. Empty plots of land, including parts of Figges Marsh and Lower Green, were used as allotment gardens, and large tracts of the Common were ploughed by Land Army girls for the War Agricultural Committee, producing crops of potatoes and cereals.

The old National Schools – the 'parish rooms' – on Lower Green West were pressed into service as the Food Office, issuing ration cards and dealing with other wartime documentation, whilst the Womens' Voluntary Service, amongst their many activities, dispensed dried milk and baby foods from their 'shop' at Fair Green. Highlights many still recall were Spitfire Weeks or the 'Wings for Victory' campaign, (with a crashed Nazi bomber on display at the Cricket Green), Home Guard and Civil Defence dances. If all else failed to lift the spirits, there was always the latest Hollywood epic to be seen twice nightly in the luxury of the Majestic Cinema at Fair Green with seats at 6d., 9d. or 1s. 3d.

The Modern Period

Post-war recovery seemed painfully slow, urgent war damage repairs being curbed by building licences, and the continuing shortages of essential materials exacerbated by the needs of the export drive. Much effort was directed by the Borough Council, by now strongly left wing, to shortening the housing waiting list by the building of municipal housing to rent. Private estates left unfinished in 1939 were completed by the Council in Wide Way and on the Brookfields estate, temporary use was made of the gunsite hutments after they had been occupied illegally by squatters, and a large estate of Arcon prefabricated bungalows was laid out on the old Pollards Hill golf course. Prefabricated two-storeyed houses – a very new venture – were also erected on the Pollards Hill estate and in Morden Road. More conventional building followed, housing estates being developed at Short Bolstead and off Tamworth Lane, followed by prestigious schemes involving medium-rise maisonette blocks at the Elm Nursery and Pollards Hill estates. Glebe Court, Hengelo Gardens and London Road south of the Cricket Green came next, and by the early 1950s Mitcham Corporation claimed with pride to have the best municipal housing record of any authority in Surrey. During this time, apart from the rebuilding of a few private houses demolished by enemy action, no private development was permitted. The site of the old refuse destructor and tip in Homewood Road, and the adjoining streets of slum housing, were cleared in the '50s to make way for one of Mitcham's most ambitious ventures, the high rise Phipps Bridge estate, sadly doomed to become another problem within a quarter of a century.

Mitcham Common, restored to public use by the late 1940s, was still in part a delightfully rugged tract of wasteland. The scars of largely illicit gravel extraction in the 19th century had now been transformed by natural reversion into numerous ponds or areas of marshland, colonised by thickets of sallow, hawthorn, gorse and bramble. Declared 'unhealthy' by would-be improvers, large areas of these wetlands were unfortunately taken for the controlled tipping of domestic refuse by the Borough Councils of Mitcham, Croydon and Sutton in the 1950s. The resulting featureless 'reclaimed' areas, and the offensive effluent that seeped from their margins, brought forth a storm of protest which regrettably was too late to have any real effect, and much of ecological interest on the Common was lost. In the main only the golf course, which many had resented strongly when it was established in 1891 for an exclusive private club, remained unscathed and retained flora typical of acid heathland.

Under the provisions of the London Government Act 1963 the Borough of Mitcham was merged with the Borough of Wimbledon and the Urban District of Merton and Morden to form the London Borough of Merton in 1965. The long tradition of truly local government was thereby broken, and inevitably old loyalties, and much that had been achieved with popular support began to be eroded. For eight years even Mitcham Fair ceased to be held, the showmen resenting the changes introduced by the new Council, and refusing to meet the increased pitch rents proposed. Happily this particular difficulty was eventually overcome, and since 1983 the fair has once more become an annual event. Educational restructuring in 1969 completed the disappearance of the long established pattern of secondary grammar schooling started under Surrey County Council, and with it many of the traditions which had evolved over the past half century.

Even the casual visitor to Mitcham was soon to notice the decline in maintenance of the roadside flower beds which had once been such a feature of the old Borough, and the pretty Fair Green Gardens deteriorated to a vandalised waste. On the credit side one could look to the Wandle, pollution much reduced by the efforts of the Thames Water Authority and its waters once more able to support fish. There was also the new swimming pool and sports complex, built as an annex to the Canons in grounds which still give pleasure. One must also mention the Council's award-winning housing estates at Cranmer Farm and on the site of Henry Hoare's mansion on the banks of the Wandle, although the Quadrant development off Western Road is aesthetically less attractive. Long-debated town centre proposals now being implemented have the potential to transform the Upper Green into an attractive modern shopping complex if the twin problems of wilful damage and litter can be overcome. Recognition of the historic and visual interest of the area from Church Road to Commonside West came with the declaration of the Cricket Green Conservation Area in 1969, but this is now seriously under threat from the increase in traffic movement, and general population pressure which has arisen with the completion of new private housing developments off Church Road and on the site adjoining Mitcham Court.

Mitcham Faeste Gestandep (Mitcham Stands Fast) was adopted, perhaps a little self-consciously, as the town motto by the borough in 1934, and still has a validity, for despite the many changes of the last half-century, Mitcham contrives to retain its special identity amongst the urban sprawl of south London, and the essential village loyalties seem never far below the surface.

1. The ford and bridge over the Wandle on the road to Sutton, *c.*1910. For more than a thousand years the Wandle defined the boundary of the parish and later Borough of Mitcham from Goat, or Mill, Green in the south to Summerstown in the north-west. 'Wicford' or 'Wykford', the name by which Lower Mitcham was usually known during the Middle Ages, was probably derived from the river crossing, whilst the prefix 'wic' hints that the ford might have served a Roman 'vicus' or settlement in the vicinity.

2. North of Phipps Bridge, *c.*1900. Now culverted and lost to sight, the ditch in this photograph followed the course taken by the Wandle before its diversion, probably after the Dissolution, to serve mills on the site of Merton priory. The line of the old watercourse, parallel with what was Phipps Bridge Road, still formed the boundary between the Urban District of Merton and Morden and the Borough of Mitcham as late as 1965. The ruined flint structure seen here was part of the old precinct wall of the priory.

3. Palaeolithic tools from Mitcham from the Sturge collection in the British Museum. The sands and gravels underlying Mitcham were dug extensively during the late 19th and early 20th centuries, and numerous stone tools from the Lower Palaeolithic, or Old Stone Age, were recovered from local pits by collectors.

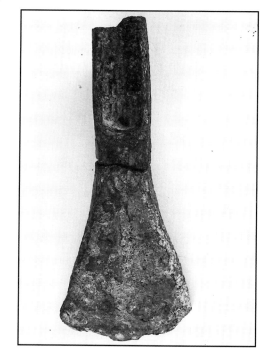

4. Neolithic Axe from Streatham Vale. This polished flint axe head was found in a brickfield at 'Lonesome' near the Mitcham/Streatham border, around 1905. Fertile and easily worked, brickearths were attractive to early farming communities, and the discovery of two other axes and fragments of Neolithic pottery elsewhere in Mitcham shows that, possibly as early as the fourth millennium B.C., the practice of woodland clearance followed by cultivation was already established in this part of the Wandle valley.

5. Bronze 'palstave' from near Mitcham Junction Station. By the beginning of the first millennium B.C. bronze was widely used for a variety of weapons, domestic implements and jewellery. Damaged axe blades such as the one illustrated are frequently found in caches or 'founders' hoards', buried near settlement areas. One such hoard, of which this tool is believed to have been a part, was found on Mitcham Common c.1890.

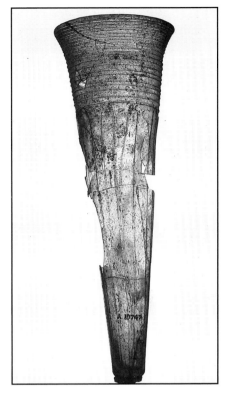

6. Roman pot from Mitcham gas works, Western Road. This intact storage jar was found at the bottom of a Roman well discovered during the construction of a gas holder in 1882. Wells are seldom far from the settlement they serve, and we can safely assume that nearby, to the west of Mitcham's Upper or Fair Green, there was a Roman farmstead or hamlet.

7. Green glass beaker from the Anglo-Saxon cemetery at Mitcham. Several items of glassware, including a Roman amphora, were recovered from the 230 or so graves excavated by members of the Bidder family between 1888 and 1922. Many more graves must have been destroyed in the past without record, and it has been estimated that the cemetery might originally have contained between 400 and 500 interments.

8. Saxon brooches from Mitcham. The Anglo-Saxon cemetery at Mitcham whence these brooches came is one of the largest known in south-eastern England. Lying either side of the present Morden Road, it was one of several dating from the mid-fifth to the late sixth century, disposed in an arc to the south and south-east of London.

9. Colliers Wood High Street, *c*.1900. Stane Street, the Roman road from London to Chichester constructed sometime around A.D. 70, continued in use as a highway long after the collapse of the Western Empire. In part its route is still followed by the A29 today. Colliers Wood High Street closely follows the line of the old road between Merton bridge and Tooting Broadway.

10. The old parish church of St Peter and St Paul. The first reference to a church at Mitcham dates from around 1170, and in 1260 the grant of the advowson, or right to appoint the parish priest, to the Southwark priory of St Mary Overie was confirmed by Baldwin de Redvers, the eighth Earl of Devon and Wight. This engraving of *c*.1790 suggests the church then standing dated substantially from the 13th century, but it may well have incorporated the remains of an earlier structure.

11. A Saxon estate boundary. At the junction of Phipps Bridge Road with Christchurch and Church Roads the Wandle, following its original course, was joined by a stream flowing westwards from Mitcham. A recital of the bounds of the estate in Merton granted by King Edgar to Earl Alphea in 967 commences 'First at Stonham and at eastern Merkepool, at Hidebourne' (the Wandle) and concludes with a further reference to the stream by 'Michamingemerke', i.e. the Mitcham border. Although one cannot be sure, the 'merke' or boundary pool seems likely to have been at this point. Certainly this was the south-east corner of the earl's estate, as it was of the later parish of Merton. The cottage to the left in our illustration, incorporating part of the precinct wall of Merton priory in its structure, was demolished with its neighbour some thirty years ago.

12. A Domesday mill site? The survey of 1086 recorded that Edmer, a Saxon, had held an estate in 'Whitford' as a tenant of King Edward the Confessor. The property included a watermill, the site of which is likely to have been near here, a little upstream from Mitcham bridge. By the 14th century there is mention of 'Wickford', or Mitcham, mill, on the site of the present Grove mill. Edmer's estate, tenure of which passed to William Fitz Ansculf after the Conquest, also included watermeadows, now part of the National Trust's Watermeads property, a corner of which can be seen in the foreground of this picture, taken *c*.1965.

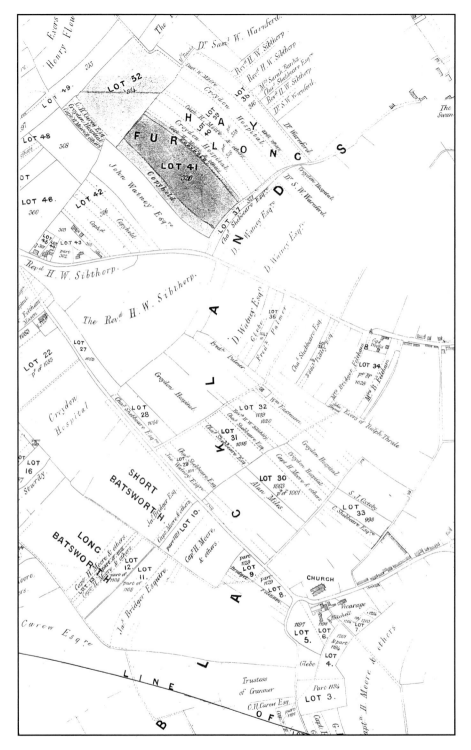

13. The 'Blacklands'. As can be seen from this map of 1853, prepared when the estate of the late James Moore was auctioned, much of the open west field of Mitcham was still farmed in strips, as it had been in the Middle Ages. The origin of the open fields (there were three in Mitcham) is unknown, but the term 'Blacklands' has in other places been found to relate to land already under cultivation during the Roman period.

14. Hall Place, Lower Green West, wash-drawing by Henderson, *c*.1820. This fascinating multi-period house, regrettably demolished in 1867, had an open medieval hall with exposed roof timbers of chestnut, a 14th-century chapel and a priest's hiding place. Excavations on the site in 1970 prior to the erection of Ravensbury School produced pottery of the 13th and 14th centuries.

15. The Hall Place archway, *c*.1972. Partially rebuilt by Sir Cato Worsfold in 1914 with stone salvaged from a medieval building being demolished on a site near Merton priory, this arch is all that remains above ground of the private chapel for which Henry de Strete, a London wine merchant, obtained a licence in 1349. The Worsfold family had preserved the arch as a garden feature in the grounds of their new Hall Place, erected in 1867. This was itself demolished in the late 1940s, but fortunately the arch has survived to become officially listed as a 'building' of historic importance.

16.   Old Bedlam, wash-drawing by J. C. Buckler, *c.*1827. This interesting building overlooking Mitcham's Upper Green was demolished around 1850. In 1789, when it was recognised as 'antique', Old Bedlam or Old Bethlehem was described as being let in tenements to poor people, but little is known of its earlier history. The jettied wings, oriel windows, and clustered chimneys suggest late medieval or early Tudor additions to an older structure. In the fenestration of the ground floor there is also a hint of an undercroft beneath an upper hall. The site is now occupied by a supermarket.

17.   Old Mitcham parish church, east end, *c.*1800. Like most English village churches, that at Mitcham was enlarged and embellished throughout the Middle Ages and the early Tudor period. The Illingworths who, it is believed, lived at Hall Place in the 15th and early 16th centuries, enjoyed burial rights at the eastern end of the north aisle, and it was possibly they who were responsible for building the chapel of Our Lady, which can be seen to the north of the chancel in this engraving.

18. 346/8 London Road, *c*.1910. Seen from the rear, the gabled roofs of this house, close by the *White Hart* and overlooking the Cricket Green, show that it is very much older than the 18th-century façade would suggest. This is confirmed by the interior, which retains a wealth of old timber beams. When this picture was taken the premises were the home and shop of Charles Matthews, barber, tailor and general draper. It is now used as offices.

19. The dovecot at The Canons, *c*.1970. Built in a chequer-work of knapped flint and dressed chalk, with thin 'Tudor' bricks at the quoins, this dovecot bears the date MCXI and obviously predates the Dissolution. It overlooks a former carp pond, and was formerly in the possession of the prior and convent of St Mary Overie, who held an estate in Mitcham and the lordship of the manor. The dovecot has been afforded the protection of official listing.

20. A 16th-century chimney-piece at The Elms, Upper Mitcham. Wash-drawing by J. C. Buckler, c.1827. One of Mitcham's larger houses, The Elms stood to the north of the Upper Green, opposite Eagle House. Parts were reputed to have dated from the reign of Edward II, and of the several elaborately-carved fire-surrounds and overmantels, one was dated 1578. During the 18th century the house was the home of the Waldos, a family of French Protestant extraction. The Elms became a private school early in the 19th century, was acquired by the guardians of the poor of the London parish of St George in the East about 1850, and was finally destroyed by a fire in 1891.

21. Mitcham Grove, c.1790. When the site of Mitcham Grove was being prepared for the erection of the present Watermeads housing estate in 1974, the foundations of a medieval house were uncovered. It is known that in the 16th century Mitcham Grove was the residence of Thomas Smythe, 'Clerke of ye Greencloth' to Queen Elizabeth I, and that it remained in the hands of his descendants until the mid-18th century. The house and grounds were presented by Lord Clive of India to Alexander Wedderburn K.C. (later Lord Loughborough) in 1773 in recognition of his spirited defence of Clive before the House of Commons, and was purchased by Henry Hoare the banker in 1786. The last owner of the house was Sir John Lubbock, and whilst in his ownership it was demolished, in the 1840s.

22. John Donne's house at Mitcham. Gallant, adventurer, poet and later Dean of St Paul's, John Donne lived with his wife and children in Mitcham from 1605 to 1611, renting a small house which he described variously as his 'little hospital', his 'prison' and his 'grave'. The house was demolished c.1846 and its site has been forgotten, but this little sketch was made of it by a Mitcham vicar, Richard Simpson.

23. The *King's Head*, London Road, c.1905. Renamed The *Burn Bullock* in memory of the popular local cricketer who held the licence from 1941 to 1954, the *King's Head* once displayed a portrait of Charles I on its sign. The counterpart of an early 17th-century lease was displayed in the oak panelled saloon, and the rear of the inn, tile-hung and gabled, is of the late 16th or early 17th century. The front, three-storeyed and 'Georgian', dates from about 1760, when it was a coaching inn of importance. Alteration of the eaves and the provision of a cornice in 1911 changed the external appearance somewhat, but false windows on the north and west elevations (to avoid payment of tax) have never been replaced.

24. Sir Julius Caesar Adelmare (1557-1636) was Master of the Rolls under James I, and is
remembered locally for the hospitality he offered Queen Elizabeth I in 1598, on one of her five visits to
Mitcham. Details of his entertainment (at great expense) of Her Majesty and her entourage have come
down to us. Sir Julius Caesar's mansion, which stood roughly where Baron Grove now joins the London
Road south of the Cricket Green, survived in part until *c*.1790.

25. Vine House, Lower Green West. According to the late Tom Francis, a local historian, the remains of a 'Cromwellian officer' were found in the garden of this house, and were re-interred in the parish churchyard. Who the officer was we do not know, but Vine House itself would appear to have dated from the mid-17th century. In the late 19th century, after several years as a private school, it was the home of William ('Billy') Hills, the last beadle of Mitcham. The house was pulled down c.1932, and the site is now occupied by a police housing estate, appropriately named Vine House and Beadle Court.

26. The Cranmers, rear view, c.1900. At the outset of the Civil War the then Rectory House was the home of Robert Howard, who was knighted by Charles I for gallantry on the field of battle near Newbury in 1644. During the Commonwealth the property was purchased by Robert Cranmer, an East India merchant, who also acquired the advowson of the church, the lordship of the manor of Mitcham, and an extensive estate in and around the village. Unfortunately Cranmer was not long to enjoy the position of squire of Mitcham for he and his wife died in 1665, leaving the estate in trust for his seven young sons. The site of the house is now occupied by the Wilson Hospital.

27. The Canons, Madeira Road, 1971. Robert Cranmer's son John, who inherited the estate on the death of his older brother (allegedly murdered by one of the trustees), granted a building lease to John Odway in 1680 for a new house to be erected on the si of the old parsonage. This was another of the properties which, until 1538, formed part of the Mitcham estate of the Augustinian priory of St Mar Overie, and it may once have been held by the canons of Bayeux. The Canons, now used for various community purposes by the London Borough of Merton, remained in the possession of the Cranmer and their descendants the Simpsons, for over 250 years.

28. Eagle House, Upper Mitcham, 1971. Recognised as one of the most noteworthy examples of the architecture of the Queen Anne period to be seen in London, Eagle House is thought (from dates on the rainwater heads) to have been erected in 1705. Until sold in 1616, the land on which the house stands was part of the estate of Sir Walter and Lady Elizabeth Raleigh. The wrought-iron gates at the front bear the initials of Sir James Dolliffe, a London merchant and founder director of the South Sea Company. In its long history the house has been the residence of city bankers, a private boarding academy, and a school run by the poor law authorities. It was sold recently by the London Borough of Merton and is now (1991) being renovated and extended for use as offices.

29. The *Five Bells*, Colliers Wood. Merton Bridge, depicted in this late 18th-century watercolour, is said to have been rebuilt in 1633, and to have had an arch 'turned with tiles', identified last century as Roman bricks. Whether or not this was so we cannot say, for the old bridge has now been demolished and a much wider bridge constructed. The old weatherboarded inn, now also replaced with a newer structure, was a regular stopping place for the carriers' wagons and stage coaches passing to and from London.

30. The *Buck's Head*, Upper Mitcham. Another old Mitcham inn, to be seen on the right in this photograph of *c*.1870, the *Buck's Head* was owned in the 17th century by the Smythe family, whose coat of arms inspired the name. The inn was one of several local hostelries used for meetings of the parish vestry before the Vestry Hall was completed in 1887. In 1895 the old inn was demolished and the present building erected. The latter was renamed *The White Lion of Mortimer* in 1990.

31. Gutteridges' shop, 29 Upper Green East, 1969. Occupying a site overlooking the Green, this old shop and its weatherboarded barns were demolished in 1970, to be replaced by a completely incongruous bank building in discordant red brick. Gutteridges was in the best tradition of a village corn and seed merchant's shop, with everything weighed and packaged in front of the customer, amidst an all-pervading earthy smell of cereals and sacking. The building itself dated perhaps to the early 18th century, but pottery found in pre-demolition excavations in the back yard showed the site to have been occupied in the 13th and 14th centuries.

32. Milestone at the corner of Lower Green West and Whitford Lane, 1868. The provision of milestones or 'finger posts' was one of the requirements of Parliament when enacting turnpike legislation in the 18th century. Two milestones survive in Mitcham, erected by the trustees for the Surrey and Sussex roads in about 1755. The stone at Figges Marsh is badly eroded, but that at the Lower Green still bears the inscription 'Whitehall 8½mls Royal Exchange 9mls.'.

33. In the early 19th century Mitcham Common, as this contemporary print shows, was well-wooded, fringed with gracious houses and private parkland, and crossed by gravelled roads. Game still abounded, and the Common also provided rough pasturage for those with grazing rights. Furze and turves were much valued by the poor as fuel, and their removal was tolerated by the lords of the manors, who were disputing amongst themselves the boundaries of their jurisdiction.

34. Millers Mead, Colliers Wood, *c.*1970. Documents of the 18th century refer to what is now Wandle Park, behind these cottages, as 'Millers Mead'. The pair of white cottages was bought in 1831 by Moses Barton Legg. a copper roller from Fareham, who was attracted by the prospect of work in the mills at Merton Abbey and migrated to Colliers Wood. The family held to the tradition that the cottage on the left had once been used by the Bow Street runners – the early police force established in the 18th century in an effort to combat highway robbery. The original Millers Mead cottages were demolished in the 1970s, but replicas have been erected in their place.

35. The *Swan* Inn, *c.*1906. The *Swan* at Figges Marsh was probably erected *c.*1808 and was intended to serve as a first 'port of call' for those travelling south through Mitcham from Streatham and Tooting. During the Epsom race week the inn was invaded by the 'fraternity' from London, but for much of the year it was a quiet country pub, frequented by tradesmen and carriers. It was extended in the 1890s, after acquisition by the Croydon brewers Nalder and Collyer. A horse trough on the forecourt was removed only recently during another 'facelift'.

36.   The Figges Marsh Gate, 1845. The turnpike gate at Figges Marsh was erected to avoid loss of revenue if the Merton gates were bypassed by those seeking to avoid payment of tolls. During race weeks the crush of impatient travellers caused many a 'scene', and attempts to circumvent the gate frequently resulted in vehicles overturning in the roadside ditch, or becoming stranded in the adjacent pond.

37.   The *White Hart*, London Road, *c*.1950. Another of Mitcham's coaching inns, the *White Hart* is recorded in a sale document of 1609, and was amongst the property purchased by Robert Cranmer, the East India merchant, during the Commonwealth. It was rebuilt in 1750, and in the late 18th century post chaises to any part of the kingdom could be hired from Holdens' stables next door.

38.   Harvesting lavender in the West Field. The commercial cultivation of lavender in Mitcham had virtually ceased before the days of photography, but this painting by Ivon Glynn conveys very well the appearance of a lavender field off Church Road at harvest time. Proceeds from the sale of 'spikings' grown on the north Mitcham estate of Merton priory formed part of the loan of £50 granted to Edward I in 1309. The first distillation of lavender water for sale in quantity is attributed to Potter and Moore, who established a small distillery in Mitcham in 1749.

39.   Potter and Moore's Herbal Distillery, c.1870. The manor house of Biggin and Tamworth and the adjoining distillery at Figges Marsh were demolished in the late 1880s, following the death in 1885 of James Bridger, the natural son of James Moore. Only two illustrations have survived of what had been one of the attractions of Mitcham, and the site is now covered by shops and the houses of Eveline Road.

40. The Willows, Willow Lane, *c*.1880. Described in 1789 as 'a good house, built in red brick', the Willows seems to have been erected in 1746 for Thomas Selby junior, a calico bleacher. The subsequent history of the property was closely linked to the industries of the area – calico and silk printing, and finally market gardening. The old house was demolished in the 1930s, but a chimney and millwheel which had served the calico printing factory were left intact for several more years, allegedly to maintain rights to water from a leat connected with the Wandle at Goat Green.

41. Wandle Villa, Phipps Bridge, 1973. Another 18th-century industrialist's house, built *c*.1789 and attributable to John Anthony Rucker, a calico printer who prospered and eventually moved to West Hill House at Wandsworth. His factory at Phipps Bridge has disappeared, but the house remains, now owned by the National Trust. Wandle Villa is a listed building, and was restored in the early 1980s after a period of neglect during which it suffered considerable vandalism.

42. Tamworth House, Manor Road. With its pedimented doorcase, five symmetrical bays and tiled mansard roof, Tamworth House was yet another typical late 18th-century house, speaking of the modest affluence enjoyed by the proprietors of the Wandle valley textile mills. Built in about 1785, Tamworth House became the home of Isaac Hillier, a partner in Howard Rivers and Co. calico printers at Phipps Bridge. During the Napoleonic War Hillier, a churchwarden, was captain of the 3rd Company of the Loyal Mitcham Volunteer Infantry. Tamworth House was bombed during World War Two, after which its shell was used for training by the Auxiliary Fire Service. What remained was demolished in the late 1940s to provide a site for municipal housing.

43. The Patent Steam Washing Factory: watercolour by Yates, 1825. This remarkable building was erected *c*.1825 on a site just upstream from Phipps Bridge. Intended to speed the processes of calico bleaching and printing, it was empty within six years of completion, a victim of the depression suffered by the Wandle valley textile industry, unable to compete with the growing Lancashire mills. After a disastrous fire in 1848 the factory was demolished, and the site has reverted to open space, owned by the National Trust.

44. Glover's Snuff Mill, Mitcham Bridge. Richard Glover appeared on the milling scene in Mitcham in about 1774, taking over the flour mill above Mitcham bridge formerly operated by Lionel Gregory. Both flour and copper milling had been the major industries here until about 1749, when copper working ceased. Glover, at first a flour miller, subsequently diversified into snuff milling, and later paper manufacture. The snuff mill in this engraving, one of several mills operated by Glover and actually situated on the Morden bank of the river, was working from about 1804 until 1834, after which it fell into disuse. It was finally demolished in 1922, but the mill race and a stone (an edge runner) can still be seen by visitors to the National Trust's Watermeads property.

45. The Ravensbury Mill, Morden Road. One of the major Wandle mills engaged in snuff milling, the Ravensbury mill, astride the Wandle, half in Mitcham and half in Morden, has a history dating back to the 17th century. Snuff milling seems to have commenced here by the mid-18th century, and in 1805 the newly-enlarged premises came into the hands of John Rutter. As Isaac Rutter and Company, the business continued under his sons and grandsons, manufacturing various tobacco products, including 'Mitcham Shag', until 1925. Unlike many Wandle mills, Ravensbury mill retained its two wheels, one of which is seen here, long after they had any practical use.

46. Mitcham Workhouse, Commonside East: watercolour by J. Hassell, 1823. Having decided to erect a new workhouse in 1782, Mitcham vestry terminated its lease of a house overlooking Figges Marsh, until then used to accommodate the parish poor. Grant of enclosure of common land was obtained from the manor of Biggin and Tamworth, and the new workhouse, erected by local builder W. Oxtoby at a cost of £1,200, was ready within the year. Following reorganisation of poor law administration, the poor of Mitcham were transferred to the Croydon Union workhouse at Duppas Hill in 1838. Ownership of the Mitcham workhouse reverted to the lord of the manor who, refusing to yield to local pressure for the site to be cleared and returned to the Common, leased the building for use as a factory. Much extended, the old workhouse accommodated a variety of industrial enterprises before being demolished during an air raid in World War 2. These included the manufacture of chemicals and lucifer matches, waterproof sheeting for troops in the Crimean War, submarine telegraph cables, and margarine and dairy products.

47. Henry Hoare (1750-1828), senior partner in Hoares Bank, Fleet Street, came to live in Mitcham in 1786. It is impossible in a few words to do justice to the immense contribution made by him to the life of the parish and the well-being of his fellow parishioners. Always ready to give advice to the Vestry, and to serve on committees, he took a prominent part in the foundation and management of the Sunday Schools and in the financing and erection of the present parish church. His memorial by the chancel arch, above his customary pew, describes him as the '... beneficent and useful life resident owner of Mitcham Grove ... a blessing and example to all around him'.

48. Mitcham Grove, c.1825. In Henry Hoare's time Mitcham Grove, beautifully situated on the banks of the Wandle, was undoubtedly the most attractive of the many substantial houses then to be seen in and around Mitcham. Mitcham had always been held in high regard as a country retreat by city merchants, bankers, lawyers and court officials, and the history of Mitcham Grove is typical. Hoare had purchased the property from Lord Loughborough, and after his death in 1828 the house and its extensive estate was acquired by Sir John Lubbock. Mitcham's popularity was by then in decline, however, and by 1846 Mitcham Grove, having failed to find a buyer, had been demolished.

49. Mitcham Sunday School, *c*.1790. Concern at the ignorance of the poor, and a desire to promulgate the basic tenets of Christianity amongst the children of the labouring classes, led to the establishment of many Sunday schools in the latter part of the 18th century. In Mitcham trustees were appointed by the Vestry in 1788, and a school for the accommodation of 150 children was erected by public subscription on land off the Lower Green donated by Mrs. Sarah Chandler. From its opening the school proved highly popular, and overcrowding soon became a problem. The Sunday School also attracted the generosity of several of the wealthier parishioners of Mitcham. An inscribed bell was donated by Mrs. Penelope Woodcock in 1791, and the following year she gave a clock, with the direction that it be fixed in a 'plain but neat manner'.

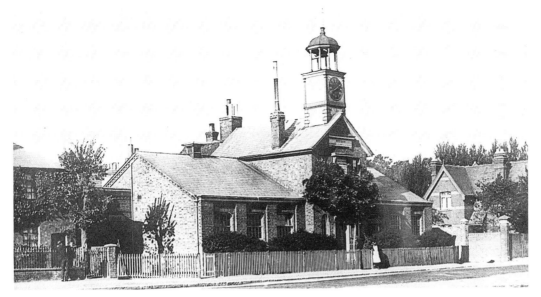

50.   The former National Schools, Lower Green West, *c*.1900. In 1812 a day school was established in the enlarged Sunday school building, under the auspices of the 'National Society for the Education of the Poor according to the Principles of the Church of England'. Extended repeatedly in attempts to accommodate the ever-increasing number of children, and after the reform of public elementary education in 1870 regularly condemned by the inspectors as insanitary, the premises continued in service as a day school until it was finally closed in 1898. The building was subsequently used, not only for the Sunday school, but also for a variety of parochial purposes, including youth activities, jumble sales and, from 1939 until 1952, as an office for the distribution of food and clothing ration cards and other war-time measures. The building, which is listed as of architectural and historic interest, was sold in 1987 by the Church, and has now been restored and converted into flats and artists' studios.

51.   The windmill, Mitcham Common, *c*.1870. Erected in 1806 on land enclosed from the Common by consent of the lord of the manor, this hollow post mill was a landmark on the Common for nearly a century. It was severely damaged by lightning in the 1860s and never restored. The mill house was rebuilt about this time, and the grounds extended, by Joseph Watson, a yeast factor. After ceasing to be a private residence it was used in the interwar period as a girls' home, and then for municipal housing, whilst outbuildings have been used as a biscuit-packing factory and changing facilities for teams using sports pitches on the Common. The base of the mill, in which the pivotal post was anchored by massive cross-beams, was allowed to deteriorate beyond repair by the owners, the local authority, and the future of both the house and the enclosed land is currently (1991) under discussion.

ROYAL SURRY MILITIA.

THIS is to certify, that at a Court of LIEUTENANCY, holden at *Croydon June y.* *First 1793* that *Thomas Ward* — — — was duly sworn and enrolled to serve as a Substitute in the above Regiment, for *Mr. James Moore* of *y. Parish of Mitcham* and that the said *Thomas Ward* — is now in actual service with the *Col. Regiment on Lig.t Comp.y of the above Reg.t at Battle Barracks* in the County of *Sussex* — Given at *Battle Barracks* — this *Third* — Day of *June* 179*8* *Tho.s of his Thompson Cap.t*

52. The Royal Surrey Militia. Like other towns and villages throughout the kingdom, the parish of Mitcham was required to provide men to serve full-time in the Navy and the Militia, or to pay a fine. Substitutes were permissible for men selected for the draft, and James Moore contrived to avoid service in the regular army by providing a substitute in the person of Thomas Ward. We know much of Moore's subsequent life, but Ward's fate is unknown.

MITCHAM,
30th. July, 1803.

THE Inhabitants of this Parish and Neighbourhood are requested to meet on MONDAY next, the First of August, at 7 o'Clock in the Evening, in the Vestry Room of this Parish, to consider further of forming

An Armed Association,

for the more effectual Defence of the Country.

ISAAC HILLIER,
THOMAS BENNETT, } CHURCH WARDENS.

Printed by T. HARDING, Croydon.

53. Stiffening the Sinews, 1798 and 1803. Although 50-odd miles from the nearest Channel coast, Mitcham responded with patriotic fervour in 1798 to the threat of invasion by Napoleon, raising funds by public appeals and forming a small force of cavalry and infantry. Another 'Armed Association' – the Loyal Mitcham Volunteer Infantry Corps – was raised in 1803, when hostilities with France were resumed. At its peak it could muster 168 officers, N.C.O.s and men in three companies under James Moore, their major commandant. The Volunteers saw no action, and were stood down in 1813 as the war moved towards its end.

54. Mitcham Church, *c.*1830. Quite apart from the structural condition of the old medieval church, which was giving rise to concern towards the close of the 18th century, the seating capacity was manifestly inadequate for the growing population. War delayed action, but in 1819 the decision was taken to demolish and rebuild. The new church, in 'Commissioners' Gothic' to the design of George Smith, was erected on the same site by John Chart, a local builder and funeral undertaker who, like his father before him, was parish and vestry clerk. The church was consecrated and opened for worship in 1822 by the Bishop of London.

55. James Dempster (1765-1821). Principal of the Baron House Academy, Dempster was also a visiting master at Glebelands, another of Mitcham's preparatory boarding academies, run by the Revd. Richard Roberts. William John Monson (1796-1862), sixth Baron Monson and one of Roberts' pupils between 1804 and 1809, before proceeding to Eton and Oxford, recalled Dempster as 'the most remarkably fat man except Daniel Lambert I ever saw'.

56. Baron House, Lower Mitcham, 1814. Once the home of Sir Thomas and Lady Margaret Blanke, where Queen Elizabeth I stayed briefly in 1591 and again in 1594, Baron House had a succession of occupants during the 17th and 18th centuries including William Farrand, doctor of law, and John Highlord and John Mendes Da Costa, both of whom were London merchants. Oliver Baron, a barrister who gave his name to the house, lived there between 1767 and 1786. By 1798 it was a boarding academy for young gentlemen run by James Dempster. The house was demolished around 1826, and the site is now occupied by blocks of Council maisonettes.

57. The obelisk, Madeira Road, 1971. The early 1820s were marked by exceptionally low rainfall in Mitcham, as a consequence of which the level of water in the shallow wells, on which the majority of households relied, dropped alarmingly. Many suffered hardship, and some resorted to the Wandle, but the water had an unpleasant taste and tended to be polluted. The appearance of a natural artesian spring in the grounds of The Canons was therefore seen as little short of miraculous, and the occurrence was duly marked by the Revd. Richard Cranmer, son of the lord of the manor of Mitcham, by the erection in September 1822 of this monument, suitably inscribed with passages from the Bible.

58. Glebelands, Love Lane, 1841. In 1793 the Revd. Richard Roberts, third son of Dr. Roberts, the provost of Eton and recently graduated from King's College, Cambridge, moved with his young wife to the newly-built villa overlooking the glebelands of Mitcham. There he established a highly-regarded boarding academy for young gentlemen which was to give a preparatory education to the heirs of several of the great families of the country. The sons of Lord William Russell, the Marquis of Exeter and his brother Lord Thomas Cecil, the sons of Baron Auckland, and the Hon. William Cholmondeley who became the third marquis and hereditary Great Chamberlain of England, all received their grounding in the classics at the hands of Richard Roberts. Perhaps best known of all his pupils were Edward Stanley, 14th Earl of Derby and Prime Minister in 1851 and 1853, and Dr. Edward Pusey, leader of the Oxford Movement, who became Lord Pusey, and had such an influence on the ordering of services in the Church of England in the latter part of the 19th century. Glebelands was damaged severely by German bombing in World War Two, but was substantially rebuilt in the 1950s and now provides residential accommodation for the elderly.

59. Deeds' Mill, Willow Lane, *c*.1960. Picturesquely situated on an island created by a diversion of the Wandle, this mill seems to have been erected around 1742 for the working of copper. It was subsequently used for flour milling and then leather working, the last occupants being John S. Deed and Sons Ltd., curriers. Little of the old mill buildings remains, and the great wheel was removed after the river was diverted in flood control works during the mid-1960s.

60. The Surrey Iron Railway at Colliers Wood sketched by Hubert Williams. The first public railway to receive Parliamentary sanction, the Surrey Iron Railway was opened to traffic in 1803. The track consisted of l-shaped short iron plate rails mounted on square stone sleeper pads, and ran from the mouth of the Wandle at Wandsworth through Mitcham to Pitlake in Croydon. Revenue was derived from tolls levied on users of the track. Never a financial success, the Surrey Iron Railway was dissolved by an Act of 1846, the land being sold back to owners of the adjoining properties. The tollgate keeper's cottage at Colliers Wood survived until after World War Two on a site opposite the Underground station. 'Tramway Path', to the south of Mitcham station, is close to the course followed by the old railway, and the present Wimbledon to Croydon line beyond Mitcham Junction follows the track exactly.

61. The White House, Cricket Green, *c*.1974. 'Ramornie', or The White House, is an attractive listed Grade II house, with origins in the late 18th century. In about 1817 it became the residence of Dr. Alfred Collett Bartley, a local doctor, and his Spanish-born wife. It is almost certainly to Dr. Bartley that the application of stucco rendering and classical porch should be attributed, and the Vestry minutes record the good doctor being reprimanded in 1820 for attempting to increase the size of his front garden by fencing off part of the Green. After the death of local M.P. Sir Cato Worsfold in 1936, The White House became the residence of Lady Worsfold, still remembered for her dedication to local affairs and in particular her wartime work with the Women's Voluntary Service and for the Girl Guide movement.

62. Elm Lodge, 1972. Another delightful Cricket Green property in the Regency idiom, Elm Lodge was erected, it is believed, in about 1807 by Edward Tanner Worsfold, a local maltster. For almost the whole of its existence it has been occupied by local doctors. Like The White House, Elm Lodge is an important element in the Cricket Green Conservation Area, and is also listed as a Grade II building of architectural and historic importance.

63. The Firs, Upper Green, c.1900. Built in about 1788 for a George Brooksbank on the site of a 17th-century house occupied by Charles du Bois, the grounds of this house inherited the remarkable collection of exotic botanical specimens brought back for du Bois by returning ships of the East India Company, of which he was treasurer. The new house was shielded from view by a high brick wall, which offered a degree of seclusion which suited the Langdales, the first residents, who were Catholic and maintained a small chapel for family use in the privacy of their own home. Langdale's father had owned the distillery in Holborn, the sacking of which in the anti-Catholic Gordon riots of 1780 was described by Dickens in *Barnaby Rudge*. After the Langdales the house was occupied by various well-to-do families until the imminent extension of the tramways to Mitcham gave what was then known as Elmwood, together with its extensive grounds, a development potential. The house was demolished in 1903, and the Elmwood Estate of largely Edwardian shops and houses now occupies the site.

64. First edition Ordnance Survey Map. This, the first accurately surveyed map of Mitcham, published by the Ordnance Survey in 1816 to the scale of one inch to one mile, shows Mitcham as a large sprawling village, extending for about two miles along the turnpike from Tooting to Sutton. Of particular note is the large Common, the 'Iron Road Way', the numerous mills and the 'calico grounds' in the vicinity of Willow Lane.

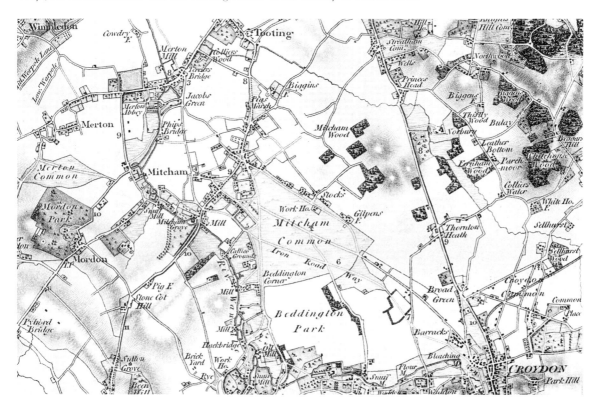

SURREY, nine Miles from LONDON

Particulars

OF

A VALUABLE AND MOST DESIRABLE

FREEHOLD AND COPYHOLD ESTATE,

(Exonerated from the Land Tax,)

CONSISTING OF

The Capital and very Substantial Residence

OF

MARMADUKE LANGDALE, ESQ.

PLEASANTLY SITUATE

AT MITCHAM,

IN THE COUNTY OF SURREY,

Only Nine Miles from LONDON, and within an easy Distance of several PACKS of HOUNDS;

WITH ALL REQUISITE

ATTACHED AND DETACHED OFFICES,

Coach Houses, Stabling, Billiard Room,

PRIVATE CHAPEL,

Conservatory, Hot House, Grapery, Lawn, Pleasure Grounds, Garden,

AND

TWO PADDOCKS OF EXTRAORDINARY GOOD MEADOW LAND,

THE WHOLE COMPRISING ABOUT

SIXTEEN ACRES.

WHICH

WILL BE SOLD BY AUCTION,

BY

WINSTANLEY and SONS,

AT THE MART,

OPPOSITE THE BANK OF ENGLAND,

On TUESDAY, the 11th of JUNE, 1822,

At Twelve o'Clock.

To be viewed by Tickets only, which with Particulars may be had of Mr. WILLIAM WITHAM, Jun. Solicitor,
Gray's Inn Square; and of WINSTANLEY and SONS, Paternoster Row. Particulars also
at the Inns at Croydon, Beddington, Carshalton, Sutton, Mitcham, and Tooting;
and at the Place of Sale.

---

65. Marmaduke Langdale's Notice of Sale, 1822. The depression following the end of the Napoleonic wars is reflected in the number of sales of Mitcham estates which took place in the early 1820s. Colliers Wood House, Biggin and The Firs were all auctioned in 1822. Langdale himself seems to have been in partnership in the Merton Abbey mills of Newton Langdale and Company, and was only saved from bankruptcy in 1820 by his brother, a partner in the Wandsworth distilling firm of Leader, Attlee and Langdale.

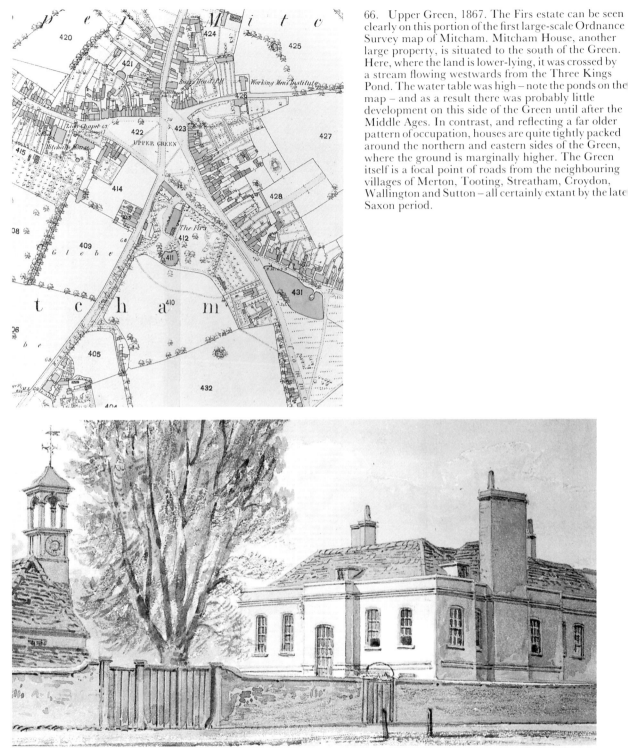

66. Upper Green, 1867. The Firs estate can be seen clearly on this portion of the first large-scale Ordnance Survey map of Mitcham. Mitcham House, another large property, is situated to the south of the Green. Here, where the land is lower-lying, it was crossed by a stream flowing westwards from the Three Kings Pond. The water table was high – note the ponds on the map – and as a result there was probably little development on this side of the Green until after the Middle Ages. In contrast, and reflecting a far older pattern of occupation, houses are quite tightly packed around the northern and eastern sides of the Green, where the ground is marginally higher. The Green itself is a focal point of roads from the neighbouring villages of Merton, Tooting, Streatham, Croydon, Wallington and Sutton – all certainly extant by the late Saxon period.

67. The Tates' house, 1827. Several illustrations of this house survive, although it was demolished in 1828. Occupying a prestigious site on the southern side of the Cricket Green, the house would appear to have dated from the early 18th century, but could well have incorporated an older building. The two Tate brothers, William and Benjamin, were active in Vestry affairs during the 18th century, and their monuments, together with those of other members of the family, can still be seen in Mitcham church. The family motto, 'Thincke and Thancke' which appears over the central door of the almshouses with their coat of arms, says much for their philosophy. For the last four years or so of its life the old house, re-named The Recovery, was used as a private nursing home for the mentally feeble.

68.   Tate Almshouses, Cricket Green, 1830. Designed by John Buckler in a modified Tudor style, the Tate almshouses were built in 1828 on land formerly occupied by the Tate family's Mitcham house. Finance was provided by the generosity of Miss Mary Tate, the surviving member of the Mitcham branch of the family, whose seat was at Burleigh Park, Northamptonshire. Miss Tate stipulated that the 12 tenants should be elderly women of good character, regular communicants of the Church of England, and never to have been a charge on the parish. Ownership of the almshouses has passed recently from trustees to the Family Housing Association, and modernisation is currently under way.

69. Cricket Pavilion, *c*.1920. Mitcham's cricket pavilion dates from the early 20th century, when the still rural traffic presented no hazard. It is now most inconveniently separated from the Green by a busy urban road. Relocation of the pavilion on the Green itself is often mooted by the cricketing fraternity. However, this would undoubtedly engender vigorous opposition from the majority of local residents, for whom the Green, once part of the common waste of the manor of Vauxhall, has a significance far greater than merely providing facilities for the devotees of cricket.

70. Cricketers and spectators on Mitcham Cricket Green, *c*.1910. Tradition holds that cricket was played on the Lower Green in the late 17th century, and the first match recorded took place in 1711. In the following century many cricketers of both local and national repute had connections with the village club. This pleasant view of a game in progress is from the clubhouse balcony.

71. Mitcham fair, *c.*1900. The origins of Mitcham fair are lost, although from time to time (usually when its future has been threatened) claims have been made that its charter was granted by Queen Elizabeth I. No such charter has ever been found. There are references to the sale of 'cattle', i.e. horses, taking place in the 18th century, but this seems to have been a minor activity, and the fair then, as now, was essentially for pleasure. The Upper Green was the customary site for the fair until 1924, when it was relocated on the 'Three King's Piece'.

72. All the fun of the Fair, *c.*1910. Traditionally held on the 12, 13 and 14 August, Mitcham fair in the mid-19th century had much in common with Greenwich fair, described by Dickens in *Sketches by Boz*. Pickled salmon, oysters and gingerbread were favourite refreshments, and Richardson's travelling theatre and large dancing booths, now no longer a feature, were highly popular.

73. 'Penny for the Grotter?' Unaware of its religious significance, generations of Mitcham children adapted the custom of constructing grotto of shells and potsherds around St James's day to serve their own ends. Shortly before fair-time, stree corners and other favoured spots acquired their candle-lit shrines. Flowers provided colour, fragments of mirror and glass simulated water, and a small doll formed the centrepiece. With grubby hands outstretched, the small architects enjoined passers-by to 'Remember the grotto' in the hope of collecting money to spend at the forthcoming fair

74. Gipsies on the Common, c.1910. The approach of fair-time was heralded by the appearance in Mitcham of large numbers of gipsies and other travelling people. Many remained to take temporary work in the physic gardens, harvesting the flowers of camomile and rose buds, or cutting the peppermint and lavender. A few eventually settled in the village, and several old Mitcham families proudly claim Romany ancestors.

75. The closing years of the 19th century and the decade prior to the outbreak of World War One provided several opportunities for national celebration, in which Mitcham people joined with enthusiasm. Charlie Matthews, tailor, barber and keen amateur photographer, had a shop overlooking the Cricket Green which is here seen resplendent in decorations to celebrate the coronation of King Edward VII.

76. Coronation procession, 1901. A popular element in any village celebration was (and still is) the procession of elaborately-decorated vehicles. Here we glimpse part of the cavalcade celebrating the coronation of Edward VII turning into the London Road by the *King's Head* inn.

77.   Derby Day traffic passing the *White Hart*, *c*.1910. The annual Epsom race week brought normal life in Mitcham to a point of chaos. Schools were shut, allegedly because of the danger to children crossing the busy roads, but in truth due to absenteeism. Those children not actually making the annual pilgrimage to the Downs with their parents lined the roads to Epsom to watch the kaleidoscopic procession of fine carriages, or to scramble for pennies tossed to them by the passing racegoers.

78.   The *Royal Six Bells*, Colliers Wood, *c*.1960. One of the favourite ports of call for racegoers on the former turnpike through Colliers Wood and Merton was the *Royal Six Bells* – 'royal' because the hostelry was patronised by Edward VII when Prince of Wales. On one occasion the prince's unpopularity prompted a bystander to throw a bag of flour, after which, it is said, he travelled to Epsom by rail. Externally the inn appears to have altered very little in the last 100 years.

79. The Sutton Road, Lower Mitcham, *c*.1870. On the right is old Mitcham Station, opened by the Wimbledon and Croydon Joint Railway Company in 1855. The building actually predated the railway, appearing as the Archway Houses in the census of 1841. The gravelled turnpike road leads towards the Lower Green, with the three-storeyed houses of Baron Row on the right and, beyond, the grounds of Mitcham Hall. Today, although its future has been debated for the last 40 years, the single track Wimbledon to Croydon line still runs a regular service, stopping at Mitcham and Mitcham Junction. The unusual station building was closed in 1988 and renovated for office use two years later.

). Old varnish house, William Latham nd Company Ltd. The commercial manufacture of paint and varnish, potentially a highly-offensive trade, became the of the main industries of Mitcham. It was established in the Phipps Bridge area *c*.1828, the of the first manufacturers being William arland. Latham's works, off Western oad, were in operation by 1851 and this arnish house, with its distinctive chimneys nd cowls, although disused, could still be en on the premises in 1965.

81. A Harland family group, c.1880. From small beginnings in the late 1820s William Harland created a highly successful business, exporting paints and varnishes to all parts of the world. Homefield, the house at Phipps Bridge built in the 1860s by his son Robert in the florid Victorian Gothic style, was an artistic wonder, decorated internally by craftsmen brought specially from Italy. Like many of his contemporaries Harland lived 'over the shop', and only the landscaped grounds of Homefield, now incorporated into the playing field of the Harland Primary School, separated him from his works. Robert Harland died in 1892 and his red marble tomb is in Mitcham churchyard, close by the front door of the church. The house has long since gone, and the site was developed for housing in the 1930s. Manufacture ceased some thirty years later.

82. The Phipps Bridge Area, 1897. Part of the 25 inch to one mile Ordnance Survey map, showing the Harlands' 'Japan and Varnish' factory and Homefield, the family residence. Note the various diversions made to the Wandle to serve old watermills or to feed the ornamental waters in the Harlands' gardens, and an old crofting ground, easily distinguished by the characteristic parallel ditches, used for the bleaching of calicos and other textiles.

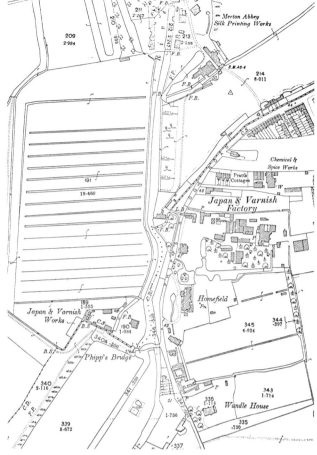

83. Firing the vats – William Harland and Sons Ltd., *c.*1920. Harlands' works at Phipps Bridge occupied the land on which the houses of Brangwyn Crescent were erected in the 1970s and '80s. Successful manufacture of paint and varnish in the 19th century relied on a high degree of experience and skill, and also much manual effort. Here we see the method of heating the 200-gallon boiling coppers, using coke fires in movable trollies.

84. Everett's Place and the Folly, Phipps Bridge, 1971. The original tenants of this row of cottages, four of which were erected in 1824 by a Henry Everett, were probably workers employed at the bleaching works or silk mill that stood to the rear, on the banks of the Wandle. Next to the left-hand cottage there was once a beer house, the *Running Horse*. The Gothic tower at the opposite end of the terrace was erected *c*.1875, allegedly to act as a buttress for the fifth cottage, which was in danger of collapse. It is also claimed that the masonry had once been part of old London Bridge. The folly and cottages are now owned by the National Trust.

85. A Wandle backwater, *c*.1900. The view behind Everetts Place in the early years of this century, showing the artificial watercourse constructed by calico printer John Anthony Rucker in 1769 to ensure a head of water for his mill. Rucker's 'new cutt' has long since been diverted to alleviate flooding, and the cottage gardens extended. The turret of the Harlands' Homefield can be seen above the trees, behind the roof and chimneys of the lodge.

86. Western Road, *c.*1906. Formerly Western or Merton Lane, this road connected Upper Green, Mitcham, with Colliers Wood, passing through what remained of the open west field and hay furlongs of the village. For much of its length it was bordered by a deep ditch, draining to the Wandle. Here can be seen the gas works (established in 1849 by the Mitcham Gas Light and Coke Company) where in 1882 a Roman well was discovered. The tall building on the left is part of the Chemist's Aerated Mineral Water Association's 'Raven Spring Works', where soft drinks were produced with water from an artesian well 233 ft. deep.

87. Pain's firework factory, Eastfields. In 1872 James Charles Pain, firework maker of Brixton, purchased a site at Mitcham, and there established a factory which flourished for 90 years. This engraving of the mid-1870s shows the works at a time when the firm was already enjoying considerable royal patronage and had acquired a world-wide reputation.

88. Watercress beds at Colliers Wood, *c*.1900. Christchurch, consecrated in 1874, is seen here from across the cress beds which extended along the eastern bank of the 'Pickle Ditch' south of Merton Bridge.

89. Mizen Brothers' Elm Nursery, *c*.1914. In the 1860s Edward Mizen, a market gardener from Battersea, acquired much of what had been the east field of Mitcham. Here, and at their other Mitcham nurseries, the Mizens raised flowers, vegetables and bedding plants for the London markets. Much of their produce was grown under glass. For virtually a century the business flourished in the hands of various members of the family, including Edward Mizen's three sons, who were foremost amongst the several horticultural growers based in the district. The Mizens' main retail outlet in Mitcham was at their Elm Nurseries in London Road, which occupied the site of the old medieval Pound Farm.

90. William Mitchell, one of the last of the Mitcham lavender workers, photographed early in the 20th century. The cultivation of lavender, albeit on a greatly reduced scale, continued in Mitcham until the early 1900s. The age of the large commercial growers had long since passed, however, and the lavender fields which remained were cropped by smallholders, selling to the London markets or itinerant hawkers who sold from door to door.

91. Peppermint *en route* for the stills, *c*.1910. This was one of the main crops of Mitcham growers like James Arthur of New Barns Farm, and cultivation was continued into the early 20th century by J. and G. Miller to the south of Mitcham Junction. The New Barns distillery was taken over *c*.1871 by Piesse and Lubin, and passed subsequently to another French firm, John Jakson and Company. The fields extended beyond the Mitcham boundary into Croydon, where the distillery was situated. The crop was cut with small hand sickles and carried from the fields wrapped in mats of sacking.

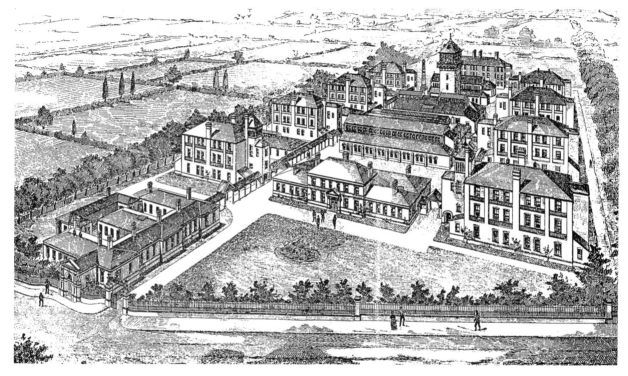

92.   The Holborn Union Workhouse. Built by the Guardians of the Poor on a 'green field' site off Merton Lane in 1886 to accommodate 1,000 paupers, the workhouse was pressed into service as a military hospital from 1916 to 1919, and was then used to house refugees from the Russian Revolution. It became an industrial estate between the wars, and the last buildings were demolished during redevelopment of the site in the 1980s.

93.   The tramway interchange, Colliers Wood, c.1910. The opening of Tooting station in 1868 and Tooting Junction in 1894 had exposed north Mitcham and Colliers Wood to the aspirations of the speculative builder. Streets of 'byelaw' houses spread inexorably southwards over the parish borders and by 1900 Mitcham north of Figges Marsh had been transformed into a Victorian suburb. The extension of the London tramway network, first to Colliers Wood and then to Mitcham itself, hastened the urbanisation process. Where Blackshaw Road met Longley Road, trams of the London County Council, using an underground conduit system, had their terminus, and passengers for Merton and Wimbledon transferred to the cars of the London United Tramways, running along Colliers Wood High Street.

94.   Streatham Road, Mitcham, c.1911. Typical of the terraces of shops built to serve the new housing estates was the Grand Parade in Streatham Road. The Ballards Estate of Caithness Road and Melrose and Park Avenues lay behind the shops, whilst to the north the grid-patterned roads of the Links Estate were spreading across the former Tooting Junction golf course. Towards Mitcham, Streatham Lane in the early 1900s was still rural, although following the deaths of William and Fanny Harris their fine Gorringe Park house became an orphanage, and the extensive grounds were divided, to be used variously as a home for horses, pitches for the Tooting Town Football Club, and a brickworks.

95.   Colliers Wood House, *c.*1890. This fine house was probably built *c.*1789 for Francis Barlow, 'Secondary of the Crown Office in the Court of King's Bench'. The site was that of an earlier Colliers Wood House occupied some forty years previously by Peter de St Loy, a wealthy Huguenot lawyer. In the 16th century Colliers Wood, held copyhold of the manor of Ravensbury, was the home of Nicholas Rutland, Elizabeth I's Clerk of the Catery. 'Colliers Wood' hints that charcoal burning was once an industry in the neighbourhood, but no documentary evidence survives, and certainly by the 18th century all trace of woodland had vanished.

96.   Warren Road, Colliers Wood, 1972. Building development on the Colliers Wood estate had commenced in the late 1860s, but progress was slow, and uncoordinated. In 1877 much of the remainder of the estate, divided into building plots, was auctioned by the British Land Company. In 1906 Colliers Wood House itself was demolished, and these typical Edwardian terrace houses in Warren Road were erected on the site.

97. Weatherboard and pantiles on the banks of the Wandle, 1970. Timber-framed 'clap-board' houses were once a common sight in Mitcham, and throughout north-east Surrey. Remarkably resilient, a few have survived the attacks of weather, rot, beetle and German bombing to provide a picturesque link with the past. Two of these three mill workers' cottages, overlooking the National Trust's Watermeads property upstream from Mitcham Bridge, date from the mid-18th century, and the group has probably been photographed more than any other buildings in Mitcham.

98. Mitcham Hall, Lower Mitcham. Watercolour by Yates, 1825. It is believed that this early Restoration house was built c.1660 as the residence of Alderman Henry Hampson, merchant taylor of the City of London and trustee of the Cranmer estate. It stood on land which had formed part of the grounds of Sir Julius Caesar's house. Amongst its many occupants of some distinction, one might mention Lady Diana Beauclerk, Lt. Gen. Sir Henry Oakes of the East India company, and George Parker Bidder, a brilliant mathematician, associate of George Stephenson and president of the Institute of Civil Engineers. Mitcham Hall survived, with later additions, until the late 1920s, its last owner-occupier, Sydney Gedge, dying there in 1923.

99. Lower Mitcham, c.1910. The Sutton road, looking north towards the Cricket Green, still had a very rural appearance at the beginning of the 20th century. The lodge of Mitcham Hall stood at the entrance to a drive, which led through a shrubbery to the front of the house, well back from the road. A pair of tall houses, erected in about 1805 after demolition of the last remnants of Sir Julius Caesar's Tudor mansion, are just visible in the distance, on the right.

100. Mitcham Park. Four large houses had been built on the London Road frontage of the Mitcham Hall estate by 1895, and development of much of the remainder of the estate commenced in 1898. Building was halted by the outbreak of war in 1914, and was not completed until the 1930s, after the demolition of Mitcham Hall. Some of the older houses, numbered 2-32, back onto Jeppo's Lane, a farm track once bordering the fields of Cranmer Farm. Gates hung on pairs of substantial red-brick pillars at either end of The Park were closed for one day annually to maintain the private status of the estate. A length of ornamental water, possibly the last vestige of an ancient moat, and unsuitable for house building, was backfilled to allow the erection of the lock-up garages now serving the houses in Baron Grove.

101. The Manor House, Lower Mitcham, 1961. The so-called Manor House – it seems to have acquired this prestigious title (without apparent justification) by the early 1900s – was typical of many of Mitcham's larger houses. In the main of 18th-century date, it was built on land the history of which can, without difficulty, be traced back to the 16th or 17th centuries, when it formed part of a larger estate. The similarity also extends to the occupants – merchants, lawyers or minor gentry with modest private means whose tenure was mostly by fixed lease of relatively short duration. A listed building, with several interesting features, including Flemish stained glass and many panelled rooms, the Manor House was gutted by fire in 1961, shortly after acquisition by a local builder who had assured worried conservationists that restoration was proposed. The site is now occupied by Justin Manor, a small block of offices.

102. Renshaw's Corner, Streatham Road, 1968. The two larger houses in this group of three listed buildings were erected c.1750, almost certainly by Samuel Oxtoby, a local builder, who lived here until his death in 1768. The use of heading bond is somewhat unusual. A third two-storied house, also of 18th-century date, was a dower house. A later single-storey extension was added as a school room when, as The Chestnuts, the property was used as a young ladies' boarding academy. In 1898 it was acquired by James Pain and Sons, the firework manufacturers, partly as a residence for Mr. Philip Pain, and partly as offices. Once again occupied as dwellings, the property is now owned by John F. Renshaw and Company, whose almond products and confectionery for the bakery trade enjoy a world-wide reputation.

103. Park Place, Commonside West, *c.*1970. Another listed building, Park Place still incorporates part of a mid-18th century house, although the main part of the property dates from *c.*1780, and was erected by Francis Gregg, a London attorney. Prior to 1391 the site, referred to as Almannesland, was in the possession of Sir John Burgersh. A farmhouse stood here in Tudor times, and the numerous residents of Park Place after Gregg included the Revd. William Herbert M.P., a noted botanist and linguist who became Dean of Manchester in 1840, and Lt. General Forbes Champagne of the 95th Regiment of Foot, a veteran of the American War of Independence. William F. J. Simpson, the last lord of the manor of Mitcham, also lived here for some 30 years. Park Place became a Y.M.C.A. hostel during World War One, and in 1922 both house and land were purchased by the *News of the World* as a club house and sports ground. The property was acquired as a school site by Surrey County Council in 1963 but not used, and after being renovated for a brief occupation by the Environmental Health Department of the London Borough of Merton was vacated for sale with planning consent for offices.

104. The Wandle above Phipps Bridge, *c.*1900. Although fast developing as a London suburb, with a vigorous industrial element, Mitcham retained many picturesque corners, particularly along the banks of the Wandle. In the early 20th century 'Bunce's meadow', seen here whilst still in private ownership – it was later acquired by the National Trust – presented a picture of rural tranquillity. Contrary to normal progression, the site had previously been industrial: a calico printing works, a large steam washing factory, a silk mill and a bleaching works all occupied the left bank. They had completely vanished by the 1870s, when the land was incorporated into the Morden Hall estate.

105. Commonside West, *c*.1910. By 1910 the *Windmill* public house, seen here on the left, was only some forty years old, but there is a record of an earlier beer house here in 1846. The pub stands 100 yards or so from the site of an unusual horizontal windmill which was working in the late 18th century, and it is possible this inspired the name. The weatherboarded cottages, which dated to the early 19th century, were destroyed in the blitz.

106. The Fair Green Methodist church, *c*.1910. The first Methodist chapel in Mitcham, still standing but now occupied as a dwelling house, overlooks the Cricket Green. It was opened for worship in 1789, 25 years after John Wesley had preached the Gospel to an uninterested audience on the Green, and had left in disgust. Despite its inauspicious beginnings, Methodism grew steadily in Mitcham throughout the 19th century, and in 1877 a new church was built on the opposite side of the Cricket Green. Another church, to the design of Sir A. Gelder and seen here, was erected on part of the old Elmwood estate at the Upper Green in 1908-9. It was destroyed during an air raid in September 1940, and was never rebuilt. Langdale Walk, a parade of shops built in the 1950s, now stands on the site.

107. Temperance Hall, *c*.1890. The late 19th century was marked by the growth of the Temperance Movement, which in Mitcham owed much to the Society of Friends. Prominent in the movement were the Pitt family who, having secured a modest income from their general stores, The London House, in Whitford Lane, reinvested their capital in houses to rent. They lived frugally, and their income seems to have been devoted largely to charity. This temperance hall in Western Road was one of the Pitts' many ventures to encourage abstinence and self improvement.

108. The Surrey Brewery, Lower Mitcham, *c*.1960. An artesian bore 350 ft. into the underlying chalk ensured a plentiful supply of pure water for the brewing of 'Mitcham Ales' throughout the 19th century. Early proprietors of this brewery were Bull and Peek, later Atlees, and then Thunder and Little. The interwar years saw the development of health and baby foods of all descriptions, and the conspicuous sign 'Expectant and Nursing Mothers need Lactagol' on the side of this fine weatherboarded house, formerly occupied by the brewers' manager, was erected by the new occupiers. In the 1930s the building accommodated a private school, called Ravensbury, but it was demolished after World War Two and the site used for a block of Council flats. A few of the brewery buildings survived until recently, but most have now been demolished and the site, to the south of Mitcham station, is used for storage.

109. The Vestry Hall, Lower Green, c.1975. Erected in 1887 to the design of Robert Masters Chart, the Vestry Hall became the Urban District Council offices of Mitcham in 1915 and, when borough status was granted in 1934, the Town Hall. The site had been that of the village lock-up, built in 1765 on a plot 12ft. x 20ft. enclosed from common land with sanction from the manor of Vauxhall. Harshly discordant in the centre of the Lower Green, the red brick and Mansfield stone structure has mellowed over time, and with familiarity has even acquired acceptance. When new it provided not only a focal point for the political life of the community, but also an excellent hall which became the venue for all manner of social events. The parish council staff were all accommodated within the building, as was the newly-acquired fire engine.

110. The Holborn Schools, Upper Mitcham, c.1905. The need to provide for the growing number of pauper children in their care led the Guardians of the Poor Law Union of St George the Martyr, Southwark, to erect a large complex of buildings on a site purchased in 1855 adjoining Eagle House. The development included this impressive building, which was a prominent feature of the London Road for some eighty years. The Holborn Union Industrial Schools, as they came to be called, were designed to accommodate 400 boys and girls. They functioned until the Poor Law was reformed in 1930, after which the buildings were demolished. The site is now occupied by the parade of shops and flats of Monarch Parade.

111. The Holborn Schools Band. The impressively-uniformed band of the Holborn Schools, some of its diminutive members carrying instruments almost as big as themselves, was much in demand at local fêtes and was an essential element in all village celebrations both before and after World War One. Here the boys are seen in the grounds of St Benedict's hospital, Tooting, where they had been performing in the summer of 1922.

112. Benedict Primary School – the *Star* School, 1973. Mitcham local school board responded quickly to the challenge of the Education Act of 1870, erecting its first school, for infants, in Christchurch Road in 1874. Killick's Lane girls' school (now St Mark's Primary) followed in 1884. The continuing need to provide better provision for elementary education led the local school board to erect this new building for 890 children in Church Road in 1897. Dubbed inevitably the *Star* School, after the nearby public house, the school drew children from the Church Road area of Mitcham and from the slums of Phipps Bridge. As a result it acquired a particularly 'rough' reputation. Still used by the Merton Education Department, it is now officially known as 'Benedict Primary School', but the old name persists.

113. Mitcham Junction station, *c*.1905. Mitcham's only main line station, affording direct access to London and the coast, was opened in October 1868 on the Balham spur line connecting the London, Brighton and South Coast Railway Company's South London line to Sutton with the Wimbledon to Croydon line of 1855. Electrification came in March 1929. A mile from the village centre, and in the middle of Mitcham Common, the station was hardly conveniently situated, and had little effect on the development of the township. It still has about it the atmosphere of a country station.

114. The 'Seven Islands' pond, Mitcham Common, *c.*1975. During the latter part of the 19th century uncontrolled removal of sand and gravel was turning the Common into a waste of pits and rubbish dumps. Like the other ponds on the Common, the 'Seven Islands' is not natural, and originated as a series of interlinked gravel pits. It was turned to good use in the 1920s and '30s, when the water was still deep enough for boating and swimming. General lowering of the water-table by extensive surface water drainage, together with natural silting, has unfortunately now reduced the depth to the point at which pond life can barely survive.

115. The Bidder Memorial, Mitcham Common, 1965. George Parker Bidder Q.C., son of George Parker Bidder the civil engineer, was instrumental in securing the passage through Parliament of the Metropolitan Commons (Mitcham) (Supplemental) Act of 1891. A parliamentary lawyer, he had as a boy enjoyed the wide open space of the old Common, and shared with many the alarm felt at its exploitation at the hands of the railway companies and gravel diggers. The act established a Board of Conservators with authority, if not always adequate financial resources, to manage the Common and to preserve its 'natural' features. The monument to Bidder was erected by public subscription after his death in 1896.

116. The Golf Club House, Mitcham Common, *c.*1905. In 1891 the Conservators leased a large part of the Common to the Princes Golf Club, which counted amongst its members many parliamentarians and wealthy gentlemen. The course was designed by Tom Morris of St Andrews, and a large clubhouse (from the Inventions Exhibition at Kensington) was erected on railway land close by Mitcham Junction station. The exclusive nature of the club engendered much ill-feeling locally, but in 1924 the links became public. The old club house burnt down in 1933, and was replaced by the present, smaller, building.

117. Mitcham Common, from the *Blue House* Bridge, *c.*1908. The Common in the early 20th century was a largely treeless heath of some 460 acres, extending to the Croydon boundary. The old *Blue House* public house, seen here amongst a group of weatherboarded cottages of *c.*1800, was replaced by the present *Ravensbury Arms* in 1906. The name of the new inn was taken from the old manor pound, which stood nearby. The cottages were demolished in 1962.

118. London House, Whitford Lane, *c.*1910. This, the village emporium selling everything from tools and hardware to clothing and footwear, closed down early in the 1950s. Founded in 1830 by George Pitt, a draper from Islington, it was run by the Francis family from 1869. In his later years, Tom Francis junior, local historian and amateur photographer, who was born above the shop, delighted audiences with his lantern slide lectures on 'Old Mitcham'. His notes and slides were bequeathed to Mitcham Library, and form an invaluable aid to speakers giving the annual Tom Francis memorial lecture.

119.   The *Bull* Inn and Church Street, *c*.1870. The first mention of this inn is in a guidebook of *c*.1789 where, as the *Black Bull*, it is described as 'a genteel and good accustomed public house, kept by a Mr. - Sanders'. Behind the inn were the grossly-overcrowded labourers' dwellings of Bull Yard and Church Place. Some of the cottages in Church Place remained occupied until after World War Two, but they have now all been replaced with modern housing. Church Street itself (now part of Church Road) has altered less, and is still recognisable in this photograph.

120. Whitford Lane, c.1880. A century ago it was a common sight to see flocks of sheep from the Surrey downs being driven through Mitcham to graze in the London parks, or to the abattoirs. Whitford Lane was then still very much a country lane, and vehicular traffic was obviously light. The high wall surrounding the grounds of Elmwood can be seen on the right, and the Upper Green is just visible in the distance.

121. Whitford Lane, looking north, c.1880. Leading from the Cricket Green and Lower Mitcham (the medieval Wickford) to the Upper or Fair Green, this road was officially styled London Road by the end of the 19th century. On the right, past the two houses, are the trees of The Firs, or Elmwood. On the opposite side of the road Glebe Villas, six pairs of late Victorian semi-detached houses, had been built on part of the parish glebeland. They were largely destroyed by a flying bomb in 1944, and the land is now occupied by the Glebe Court housing estate of Mitcham Borough Council.

122. 'Lazy Corner' – The Upper Green, *c.*1895. The village pump, with its attendant loafers, was a favourite subject of early photographers in search of local colour. It was also the regular venue for soap box orators and the Salvation Army Band. The well was covered, and the pump replaced by the present cast-iron clock tower-cum-drinking fountain, erected (by public subscription) to commemorate the 1897 Jubilee of Queen Victoria. Note the old weatherboarded *King's Arms* on the left.

123.   The High Street, *c*.1908. It is interesting to compare this view with that seen in the preceding photograph. Widening of the High Street was considered in 1906 when the tramways were laid down, but it never took place, and even today the road narrow by the former *Buck's Head* and the terrace of shops next door.

124.   The *Old Nag's Head* and Upper Green West, *c*.1908. A rare view of the north side of the Upper Green. The original *Old Nag's Head*, on the left, had not been demolished, and the central 'green', covered annually by the caravans and booths of Mitcham Fair, supported little vegetation.

125.   Upper Green East Clock Tower, *c*.1908. Seen from this angle, the eastern side of the Upper Green has changed remarkably little in the intervening years. The open-topped tram to Croydon offered a pleasant country ride across Mitcham Common as far as Aurelia Road, where the houses of Croydon commenced. The clock tower may or may not have been showing the correct time – it stood over a disused well and the water vapour is said to have had an adverse effect on the clock's machinery!

126.   The Broadway. A view of Lower Mitcham, *c*.1906. From the *White Hart* northwards the scene is much the same after 80 years, although traffic of course has increased dramatically. A branch tramway, terminating opposite the *White Hart*, had just been constructed. The old *Cricketers*, destined to be badly damaged in an air raid in September 1940, can just be made out on the left, by the carriers' wagons. The Broadway was an important commercial area in its day, with a bank, rural district council offices, a butcher (slaughtering on the premises), grocer, dairy, bakery, tailor and so on, all grouped round the cross roads.

127.   The Causeway or Lower Green East, *c*.1906. Probably named because the roadway had been slightly raised above the adjacent green, which before proper surface-water drainage tended to become marshy in winter with water draining from the Common. The sign of the old *Britannia* (long closed) can be seen, and on the right, the 18th-century Methodist chapel, converted to a bungalow. The tall building beyond is Mitcham's first police station.

128. Cranmer Green, *c*.1906. Twelve acres of former parish 'waste', Cranmer Green or Cranmer's Piece, passed under the control of Mitcham Urban District Council in 1923, and is now maintained by the London Borough of Merton. Thompson, a local dairyman, was one of those who still laid claim to common grazing rights until about the time of World War One. The old Rectory, by the early 1900s generally known as The Cranmers, lay behind the fence on the left, whilst in the distance can be seen the lodge and wall enclosing the grounds of The Canons. Both houses were then occupied as gentlemen's residences. The pond survives, but is now usually dry; the big trees have fallen, but the scene is still easily recognisable.

129. The *Three Kings* and pond, *c*.1906. The 18th-century *Three Kings* was replaced after demolition in 1928 by a new building in the popular 'mock-Tudor' style. Whether the three kings were biblical or Hanoverian is unknown. The pond has existed for 300 years or more, and is referred to in early documents as 'Heathernderry pond' or 'The Great Pond'. It is the oldest of the several ponds on Mitcham Common, and is fed by a stream running alongside Commonside East. The outflow passes into a surface water sewer beneath Commonside West.

130. The brook at Figges Marsh, *c.*1910. The 'Little Graveney', flowing from Pollards Hill to join the Graveney itself near Tooting Junction station, was originally visible as an open stream running alongside Figges Marsh (which it often flooded). The line of the stream was for many years marked by a row of former hedgerow elms, but these were lost to disease in the 1970s, and now only the occasional manhole hints at the little river below ground. The houses in the background are on the new estate built off Gorringe Park Avenue.

131. The Wandle Fisheries, *c.*1910. Since the beginning of the 17th century the Wandle had been noted for its excellent trout, but by the late 19th century increasing pollution from the sewage farm at Beddington was causing concern. In an attempt preserve the fishing and conserve stocks, three local landowners formed the Wandle Fisheries Association, established a tro hatchery in the Watermeads and installed their bailiff, Harry Bourne, in the cottage facing the bridge. Court action against the Croydon Sanitary Authority failed to secure improvement in water quality, and by the 1920s very few trout survived. Rece attempts at re-stocking have also met with only temporary success.

132.   The Grove Mill fire, 1907. The vulnerability of mills to fire was demonstrated frequently at Mitcham, and yet in the 18th century at least two of the mills seem to have been constructed of tarred paper over a timber framing! Later mills were built of brick and slates, but fires continued to occur. The Grove mill was gutted in 1907, when it was used by Lyxhayr Ltd., a firm manufacturing upholstery filling. The upper storey was omitted when the mill was rebuilt, and it remains a two-storeyed structure today. Members of the Mitcham Volunteer Fire Brigade can be seen in this postcard with Mr. Dickinson, the manager of Lyxhayr, who is wearing a top hat.

133. Hall Place, Lower Green West and Canon Wilson's Jubilee. Flamboyantly Gothic, Hall Place was erected by William Worsfold in place of the old medieval house, demolished in 1867. In 1909 the house and grounds witnessed the Jubilee celebrations of the vicar of Mitcham's induction. Daniel Frederick Wilson M.A. of Wadham College, Oxford, an honorary canon of Southwark cathedral, held the living at Mitcham for longer than any other incumbent, dying in 1918 after 59 years' service to the parish. During his long ministry the village changed more than at any time in its history.

134. Bennetts Hole, *c*.1906. A bend in the river Wandle above the National Trust's Watermeads property was marked as Bennetts Hole on a 16th-century map of the Howard estate, and is still shown as such by the Ordnance Survey. There are also references to 'Beneytesfeld in Wykeford' as early as 1362, but neither the significance of the name nor its derivation are known. Whilst the land on the eastern bank of the river is now occupied by the Willow Lane factory estate, the opposite side is maintained as public open space by the London Borough of Sutton.

135. Mitcham Bridge. The road south to Sutton crossed the Wandle by this bridge, rebuilt in brick by the County after the parishes of Mitcham and Morden had been 'presented' in 1759 for their failure to ensure the bridge was kept in proper repair. The ford was retained, and was obviously still appreciated by the drivers of horse-drawn vehicles when this photograph was taken *c*.1906.

136. Mitcham Fire Brigade, 1922. In 1920, when Mitcham's first professional chief fire officer was appointed, the brigade boasted two vehicles, a 1911 Merryweather with a 360-gallon Hatfield motor pump, and a Dennis motor fire tender (seen here at the rear). When the parish acquired its first 'steamer' in 1884 the normal life of Mitcham came to a halt, and the villagers turned out to line the streets to welcome the new engine, a Merryweather No. 1 Volunteer, pulled by a team of horses. It was led in procession around the Lower Green by the visiting brigades from Sutton and Merton.

137. The last fair on the Upper Green. August 1923 saw Mitcham Fair held for the last time on the old Fair Green. Trams and the increasing motor traffic were making attendance at the fair extremely hazardous, and under the power conferred by the Mitcham Urban District Council Act, passed in July 1923, the fair was moved the following year to the Three Kings Piece. Apart from a short break during World War Two, and another in the 1970s, it has been held there ever since.

138. Camomile Avenue, Upper Mitcham, *c.*1925. The Urban District Council of Mitcham was in the forefront of providing 'homes for heroes' after the end of World War One, and soon after the signing of the Armistice work commenced on the first phase of a new Council housing estate off Figges Marsh. Land was still cheap, and the new estate could be designed on the garden village principle. With a touch of nostalgia, the roads were given names recalling the plants grown in the Mitcham physic gardens in years gone by.

139.   The Wilson Hospital, *c*.1975. Erection of the Wilson Hospital in Cranmer Road, on the site of the old Rectory House purchased by Robert Cranmer in 1652, was largely made possible by the generosity of Isaac Wilson (later Sir Isaac), a successful building developer. It was opened with due ceremony in 1928 by Princess Mary, the Princess Royal. The hospital became the focus of much local pride and loyalty in the 1930s, with a constant stream of donations from many local firms and individuals being received by the trustees. Voluntary contributions funded enlargement in 1934, and the annual fund-raising hospital fête at Mitcham Stadium was a regular feature of the local calendar until the war.

140.   The Cranmer Middle School, 1973. A typical school building of the interwar period, erected by the education department of Surrey County Council on the site of Cranmer Farm. A medieval tithe barn was demolished during the course of redevelopment work, and beams from the old building were incorporated in the library and the octagonal hall of the new school. The school opened as Mitcham County School for Girls, and Miss Dunn, the first headmistress, who joined the school in May 1929, remained in that post until her retirement in 1955.

141. The Explosion at W. J. Bush and Company's distillery. Events in Mitcham seldom
reached the national headlines, but an explosion in 1933 at the works of W. J. Bush and
Company, off Church Road, was an exception. One small boy was killed, 23 people were
seriously injured, and many families living in cramped Victorian cottages in the adjoining
streets were made temporarily homeless. Bush and Company were distillers of oils and
essences in the tradition of Potter and Moore, whose business they had acquired in 1888.

142. Mitcham Garden Village, 1973. Part of Rowcrofts, a meadow occupying a corner of the grounds of The Cranmers, was used as the site of Mitcham Garden Village, erected between 1928 and 1932. Construction was by Charles Higginson, a local builder, to the design of Chart, Son and Reading, and funding was provided by Sir Isaac Wilson. The houses were designed to accommodate the elderly, and today the estate is still the quiet backwater conceived by its founders.

143. The Fire Station, Lower Green West, c.1975. Until the present fire station was opened in 1927 Mitcham's No. 1 engine was housed in the Vestry Hall, whilst the second engine was stationed at Colliers Wood. The Mitcham brigade was integrated with the London Fire Service after the war, and now, although able to give a far more efficient and sophisticated service, it has inevitably lost much of the purely local appeal it once enjoyed.

144. Ravensbury Park, c.1930. The Ravensbury estate, belonging to the Bidder family, was sold in the interwar years and was rapidly disappearing under speculative housing estates when Mitcham, acting jointly with the Urban District of Merton and Morden, acquired 16½ acres on the banks of the Wandle as a public park. The handsome Manor House, built in the neo-Georgian style by Colonel H. F. Bidder on the south bank of the river (seen here), was demolished in the 1930s, and the site is now covered by houses in Wandle Road. Fragments of a far older Ravensbury manor house can still be seen in the park.

145. The Majestic Cinema, Upper Green, 1971. Ravensbury, the Edwardian 'Tudor' house occupied by James Drewett the undertaker, was demolished in 1933 to provide the site for Mitcham's one and only picture palace. Previously there had been a little 'flea pit' in London Road to the south of the Upper Green, showing silent movies, but this was before the days of the 'talkies', which brought a new world of glamour and fantasy. With the decline in cinema-going the Majestic closed down in 1961, and for the last 14 years of its life the building was a bingo hall and casino. Following demolition the site was redeveloped as a supermarket.

146.   Charter Day, 19 September 1934. The granting of Borough status to Mitcham was the occasion for much civic celebration. Charter Mayor was the 84-year-old Robert Masters Chart, an architect by profession, alderman of Surrey County Council, former Mitcham vestry clerk and holder of innumerable public offices, both paid and unpaid, over the previous 50 or more years. The Chart family's record of continuous service to Mitcham was quite remarkable, and had commenced with the appointment of Robert Masters' great-grandfather William to the post of vestry clerk in 1761.

147.   Mayoral Opening of the Fair, 1936. By the 1930s the annual opening of the Mitcham Fair on 12 August, followed by free rides for the children, had been elevated to a major event in the civic year. The preceding two centuries had seen several attempts by the authorities at actually suppressing the fair, none of which succeeded. Today, to the acclaim of the assembled crowds the 'traditional' golden key (supplied by the Showmen's Guild) is held aloft by the mayor in full regalia, signifying official consent.

148. Mitcham Court, Cricket Green, 1972. Elm Court, as it was originally known, seems to have been erected as a simple three-bay villa for Dr. John Parrott, a local G.P., c.1824. It was extended in the late 1860s by Caesar Czarnikow, a London sugar broker. The last private resident was Harry (later Sir Harry) Mallaby-Deeley M.P. who, in 1936, sold the house and its fine grounds on favourable terms to Mitcham Corporation, on the understanding that the land would be used for new public buildings. Had war not intervened, Mitcham Court could well have become the site of a new town hall. As it was, the coach house and garage became the ambulance station, and the house itself was used as offices by the Borough Housing and Public Health Departments until the property was sold by the London Borough of Merton.

149. Mitcham County School for Girls, Cranmer Road. Form 3M are seen here in the early summer of 1939, with their form mistress, Miss Marsden. The girls, most of whom were about thirteen years of age, are all neatly dressed in their summer dresses of lavender and white. Many are wearing their house shoes, which school rules demanded should be worn inside the building to protect the polished floors. Within three months their young lives were to be turned upside down: Britain was at war with Germany, fathers and brothers were being called up for the forces, and half the school had been evacuated to Weston-Super-Mare.

150.   Baths Hall decorated for the Coronation of George VI in 1937. Demolished in the mid-1980s to provide access to a new multi-storey car park, Mitcham's baths hall in London Road was another of the outer trappings of the new civic pride. It not only contained public baths, washing facilities and a modern swimming bath, but during the winter when the pool was not in use and floored over, the building served as an excellent public hall for private and public functions.

151. Mitcham Home Guard. Raised initially in May 1940 as the Local Defence Volunteers, the 57th Surrey (Mitcham) Battalion of the Home Guard were under the command of Lt.Col. W. E. Nelson M.C. Many of the men were 'old sweats' from World War One, battle-hardened in the trenches of Flanders. *Esprit de corps* was high, and although at first woefully ill-equipped, eventually they were to become a highly efficient unit, totally unlike the image of 'Dad's Army' portrayed on television. Officers and N.C.O.s of 'A' Company, under the command of Major E. L. Shepard (5th Seaforth Highlanders 1914-19) are seen here outside the battalion headquarters at the golf clubhouse, Mitcham Common.

152.   A crashed Heinkel He 111K bomber displayed on the Cricket Green in November 1940 in aid of the Spitfire Fund.

153. The *Cricketers* public house, virtually demolished by a delayed action bomb dropped in 1940.

154. Air Raid Incidents, 1940-5. Mitcham was generally considered to have been one of the most heavily bombed of the south London suburbs, and the number of 'incidents' shown on this map from the Borough Engineer's office gives some idea of the extent of the damage caused. In addition to the parachute mines, incendiaries and normal H.E. bombs dropped during the blitz of 1940-3, no fewer than 49 'V1s' or flying bombs – 'doodlebugs' – fell on Mitcham during the closing years of the war. Very few houses escaped damage, and many hundreds were either destroyed outright or had to be demolished.

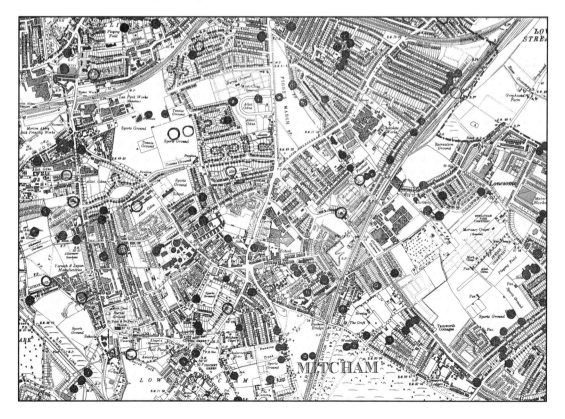

155. Blackened church interior, March 1948. Miraculously Mitcham parish church escaped serious structural damage during World War Two. Some Victorian stained glass was lost through bomb blast, in spite of sandbagging, but far more severe damage was caused to the interior by a deranged boy who gained access to the church in 1943, and started a fire in the base of the tower. The organ was destroyed, and much interior woodwork. The fire-blackened interior (seen here from the west gallery) was cleaned and redecorated in time for the Festival of Britain in 1951.

156. Unveiling the Home Guard Memorial, Tower Creameries. In 1941 a parachute mine dropped by a German aircraft fell on The Creameries on Mitcham Common, at which members of 'B' Company of the 57th Surrey (Mitcham) Home Guard were on duty. The works were set ablaze and 15 members of the unit were killed. They were buried with full military honours, and the headstones of their graves can be seen in Mitcham's London Road cemetery. In 1962 Col. S. W. Barber, Deputy Lieutenant of Surrey, unveiled a simple plaque to their memory on the new factory building on Commonside East.

157.   War Damage rebuilds, 1950. The only private house-building permitted in post-war Mitcham was of war-damaged properties. Even then, work was severely restricted in extent, and hampered by shortage of materials. In Mitcham Park clearance of an emergency static water tank on the site of a pair of substantial Edwardian houses made way for a block of eight small flats. Externally, however, the new property was a tolerable copy of that demolished during the blitz.

158.   Construction of the Pollards Hill maisonettes, 1950. Mitcham Borough Council's first high-rise dwellings of the post-war era, these blocks of maisonettes on the Pollards Hill estate were part of a mixed development, commencing with temporary but highly popular prefabricated Arcon bungalows, and continuing with prefabricated two-storey houses.

159.   Slum clearance. Priorities for post-war clearance were determined more by the need for quantitative rather than qualitative gain, and although most of Mitcham's slums had been demolished before clearance was stopped in 1939, small areas of sub-standard housing remained. These houses in Sibthorpe Road, together with the neighbouring Fountain and Gladstone Roads, were typical, and disappeared in the early 1970s to make way for the 'Quadrant' housing scheme.

160.   James Pascall Ltd., Streatham Road, 1971. For a little over 70 years Pascall's factory dominated north Mitcham. Hundreds of local people found work there, and the air in the vicinity of the works was often heavy with the scent of chocolate or boiled sweets. A disastrous fire at Pascall's Blackfriars factory in 1897 had precipitated a move to a larger site, and Mitcham was chosen for the firm's new Furzedown Works. In 1959 Pascall joined the Beecham Group, who in 1964 sold their confectionery interest to the Cadbury-Fry organisation. Rationalisation followed and within seven years production had ceased at Mitcham, and Pascall's works were awaiting demolition.

161. 'Arthur's Pond', Commonside East, 1971. New Barns farm, occupied by 'physic gardener' James Arthur in the mid-19th century, stood behind the houses seen here fronting Commonside East. They were built in the 1930s on former commonland, enclosed a century previously. The farm pond, once fed by a stream and overhung by a willow, is now a forlorn sight, more often than not dry. Attempts to rejuvenate the pond a few years ago by re-excavation and lining with plastic have been ineffective, due to a general lowering of the water table by surface water drainage.

162. The Upper, or Fair, Green, 1972. Post-war expenditure by the Mitcham Borough Council on landscaping and planting became a matter of acrimonious political controversy, despite the obvious improvement to the appearance of the Green. Always at risk of disappearing behind a growing clutter of street furniture, the Green has deteriorated in the last 25 years through a combination of municipal neglect and apparent public indifference, and is now shabby and unattractive.

163.   Industrial Colliers Wood. No longer a rural hamlet separated from Mitcham by open fields, Colliers Wood is now part of the urban sprawl of south London, with a strong industrial element. Since this photograph was taken in the early 1970s, the Savacentre supermarket and the Merton relief road – Merantun Way – have replaced many of the factory buildings to be seen to the right of the picture.

164.   In January 1637 the spire of the steeple of old Mitcham church was struck by lightning in a storm which damaged a number of Surrey churches. At Mitcham the subsequent fire destroyed the chancel roof, and the repairs were not completed until 1640. History repeated itself in 1785, when fortunately less damage was caused, and again in 1975 when, as can be seen above, a corner turret was brought to the ground.

165.   62-6 Church Road, Mitcham, 1965. By the designation of the Merton (Mitcham, the Cricket Green) Conservation Area in 1969 Merton Borough Council gave recognition to the historic and aesthetic interest of the area from Mitcham church to the Three Kings Piece. These listed houses in Church Road date to about 1740, and have recently undergone restoration.

166. The Lower Green, 1972. Two 18th-century houses and a pair of Victorian villas form an attractive backdrop to Lower Green East, or the Cricket Green, still one of the most pleasing corners of Mitcham. This view can have changed little in the last hundred years or so.

167. Cricket on the Green, *c*.1975. Another scene on the Green with a timeless quality. One has an uncanny feeling when looking at photographs taken from the same vantage point a century ago that the same match is in progress!